A tale of hurt,
healing and choice

BEHIND CLOSED DOORS

Christine Elizabeth

First published 2026 by Christine Elizabeth

Produced by Independent Ink

Copyright © Christine Elizabeth 2026

Cover design by Catucci Design
Edited by Lucy Czerwinski
Internal design by Independent Ink
Typeset in 12/17 pt Garamond Premier Pro by Post Pre-press Group, Brisbane

 A catalogue record for this book is available from the National Library of Australia

ISBN 978-1-7646587-0-6 (paperback)
ISBN 978-1-7646587-1-3 (epub)
ISBN 978-1-7646587-2-0 (kindle)

DEDICATION

To my family and friends, near and far, who fill my
life with meaning, joy and love—thank you for you.
I see, hear, connect, honour and appreciate you.

For those my book has found, this is also for you—for whenever
any of us have felt unseen, unheard, uncertain, or endured suffering.
I hope you find a sense of connection here, guiding you towards
compassion, empathy, love and healing for yourself and others.

May we all shine brightly, smile broadly, and live fully.

'Nothing is covered up that will not be revealed, or hidden that will not be known. Therefore whatever you have said in the dark will be heard in the light, and what you have whispered in private rooms will be proclaimed from the housetops.'—Luke 12:2

'Do not judge, and you will not be judged. Do not condemn, and you will not be condemned. Forgive, and you will be forgiven.'
—Luke 6:37

CONTENTS

PREFACE

2014

My heart swelled with joy. I was pumped! Enthusiasm and anticipation swept over me, and I could not help but smile eagerly. We were on our way to celebrate my youngest sister's fortieth birthday—it was a family gathering that promised to be special, just like every other celebration.

The sun shone brightly on the bonnet of our car. My partner, Angus, drove along the familiar highway to the home of one of my other sisters.

I was lost in my thoughts. I could imagine my sister Nancy, her eyes gleaming with mischief, when she reminded me that I was the oldest and that I would always be the oldest. I think she liked being the youngest and more than that, she enjoyed teasing me. Anticipating her mockery was simply part of my eagerness and excitement for the night ahead. Our family celebrations were always awesome fun, filled with sounds of laughter, the telling of tales, corks popping and the sharing of food.

What I didn't anticipate was that this celebration would not be the same as all the other parties. It was going to be the night when everything would change, and I had no idea.

I had four siblings, with just over four years between us. I was born, and then fourteen months later, my fraternal twin sisters, Jennifer and

Cynthia, were born. My brother, David, followed the next year, and then my youngest sister, Nancy—born three months early—the year after. I grew up in a very busy and, when allowed, a very noisy household.

I had four siblings, but my mother gave birth to six children. My youngest sister, Nancy, was a twin, and her sister, Antoinette, was stillborn. Hence, why Nancy was premature. I can only imagine the deep loss, sadness and grief my mother must have felt. Nancy also feels heartache, often expressed as a sense of incompleteness. I feel a deep sadness for her whenever she talks about her twin. I still consider Antoinette as one of my siblings. I will, however, for the sake of ease when reading my story, refer to my four immediate siblings and myself as the five of us.

MY SISTER

My twin sister -
The one I never grew up with,
The one I never met.

I wish she was here,
It's God's way
Of keeping the peace,
She wasn't given a life. I was.

She was given a name: Antoinette,
I was given mine: Nancy.
I have a chance
To do something with my life.
She does not.
I wish she was me.

She looks like me,
She is me.
All combined in one body.
I am Antoinette.
I am Nancy.

I am both of us,
I'm part of her,
Like she is still a part of me,
Forever.
I will not forget her.

May Antoinette Rest in Peace – Forever in my Heart.
Written by Nancy as a teenager.

I talk about my immediate siblings, but before us, my father had another family. He had three daughters before us. Lee, Elizabeth and Julie. Even though Lee was thirteen years older than me, I was close to her.

My aspiration in writing this book was to bring together my point of view and express how I interpreted the pivotal events and how secrets and betrayal changed my family in a short moment. Could I come to terms with intense changes, intrusive thoughts, all-consuming grief and sleepless nights? Such things became commonplace after my sister's fortieth birthday, prompting me to consider the impact of such a monumental transformation. What I once believed to be our family unit was no longer. Certainly, though, this experience with my four siblings enabled a far greater closeness between us.

At the beginning of this journey, I kept a journal to help me process my thoughts, feelings, emotions and grief. While it is true that, with time, some moments dwindle from memory, drafting my story with the aid of my journal has allowed me to reflect and consider those pivotal events.

Some of the journal entries I wrote in the middle of the night while unable to sleep. Journaling helped me to process my thoughts, so I could get back to sleep. Some of those words are now contained within these pages. As I re-read and wrote about them, it was almost as if I could view the scenes from my memories all over again. Other times, unconsciously, I placed myself somewhere else, like I was writing from someone else's life and perspective, not my own. At times, it was easier to do it that way.

The process of writing here has been immensely valuable to me in gaining a sense of clarity and understanding. It has helped me to increase my empathy by viewing the events objectively, the why and how. As a nurse, I have always been empathetic to others. But in this case, it became a tool for discovering the meaning of forgiveness and healing. It has allowed me to address my healing for my future. The question became: can I forgive by letting go so that I can move forward and shine the brightest?

Forgiveness is something that helps us in our journey through life. It allows us to leave behind the hurt and anger and to move forward in life with freedom and excitement. Am I capable of such forgiveness, or will that forgiveness escape me?

Ultimately, it is the surreal notion that this happens in other people's families and not in mine that I often still struggle with. It was like it wasn't us; instead, I would be watching a movie that played out in front of me. Yet, this was and is very real, and it did happen to us.

On the inside cover of my journal, I wrote the words, 'How dare you!' For a fleeting moment, I thought that could be the title of this book, but as I wrote the pages, 'To Forgive or Not Forgive' represented the story better. Forgiveness became my journey within and out of these pages.

However, in the later stages of getting my book ready for publication, the title became *Behind Closed Doors*. This title has an added meaning and a powerful connotation, since my father alluded to that when I was growing up. To Forgive or Not Forgive then became the final chapter of my book.

Writing my book has been an amazing experience. It's something that I had talked about for nearly ten years. As I fulfil my dream to write the words that make up my story, I am proud of myself for taking the steps that I needed.

I would sit and somehow my fingers knew what to write as each letter became words, words became paragraphs and so on. I'm not sure how the words flowed, but they did. I would go back and make corrections, but initially, getting the facts down was the first step. The second and third drafts were about getting the emotions, feelings and my truth onto the pages. That became harder and harder with each chapter and each draft.

When I started, I was concerned about not having enough to write about, even with the help of my journals. I only planned eleven chapters. When I had written 20,000 words, I thought that it would be completely unfathomable and inconceivable for me to write 30,000 words. But as I continued to write, I realised I had much more to say.

What I still find even more remarkable is the birth of chapters sixteen and seventeen. They were hard and often emotional for me to write. But, somehow, I knew that there was a bigger purpose as I wrote those pages. What I didn't realise at the time was that I'd begun my own personal chapters of forgiveness and healing. It had become a very cathartic journey.

We all have our own stories. Many of those born around the same time as I was, will have similar notions about their upbringing. Some will be happier, others sadder and more tragic. Whatever your story, whenever you were born, whatever your upbringing, wherever life has taken you, and whatever your financial status, culture or beliefs, I hope you can resonate with my words. For this is my story.

MY FAMILY TREE

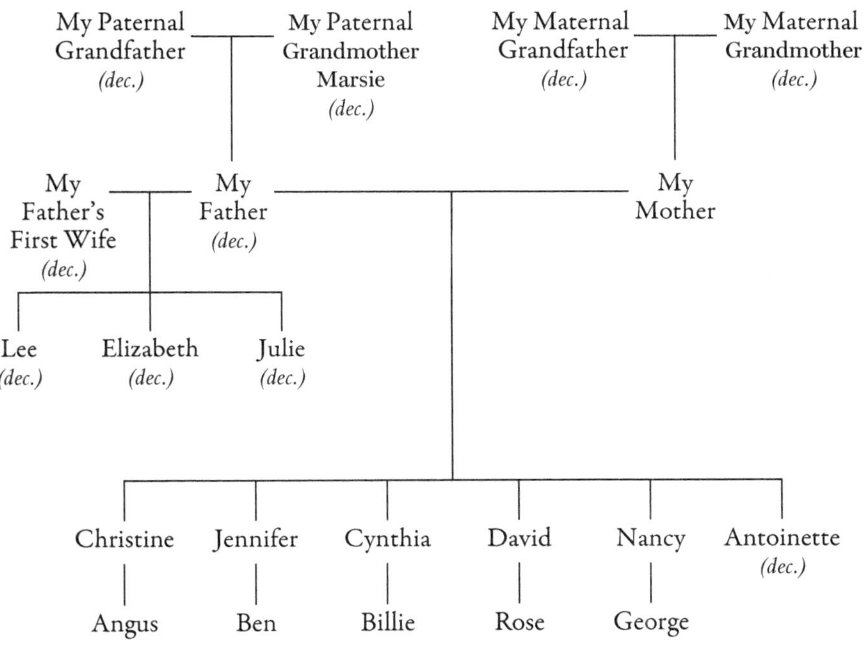

YOU'VE GOT FAMILY

When you love the ones you love,
You've got family,
All you have to do is call,
And they'll be there.

Family is a privilege,
For those who cherish it right.
Respect is a privilege,
For those who earned it right.

When you treat them well,
They'll treat you well.
When you are true to them,
They'll be true to you.

If you're down and out,
They'll be there for you.
If you need guidance,
They'll be there for you.

When times are happy and joyful,
They'll be there with you.
To see the excitement and smiles
They'll be there with you.

Cherish them when you see them,
Cause they'll certainly see you.
Cherish them when you hear them,
Cause they'll certainly hear you.

So, treasure each moment,
When they rush to be with you.
So, treasure each moment,
When they burst through the doors to be with you.

'cause one day it'll all be gone,
In the blink of an eye.
'cause one day you'll not do them right.
In the blink of an eye.

Family is a privilege,
But don't go disrespecting.
And don't go forgetting,
Cause they'll remember when you call.

When you love the ones you love,
You've Got Family.
All you have to do is call,
And they'll be there.

PART ONE

BEGINNINGS

Chapter 1

REMINISCENCES

Life is a journey full of memories—some remembered,
some treasured, some forgotten, and others reminiscent
of a sunrise that did not shine brightly.

My tale seemed normal, yet it was not. It was the era of different ideals and enforced notions of morality. But was it right or wrong, and who determines that? Regardless, the brunt of past ideals can be passed on to future generations. Would my siblings and I bear the brunt of past lies and secrets? And is it conceivable that we were never meant to know?

Memories play a crucial role in shaping our sense of identity, our ideals and our sense of right and wrong. However, they can be flawed, leading to challenging questions. I was beginning to feel that I didn't have a sense of identity, but maybe I was about to find it. To unravel this mystery, let's delve into the memories and reminiscences, those that shone brightly or not.

As a five-year-old, I remember walking to school with the children from next door. I was friends with one of my classmates, the boy next door. I can still picture walking to school on our first day, with him and his two older sisters, just us, no parents or adults. The trees lined the sides of the road, and we walked in the middle of the road. Our very own guard of honour made of trees.

We lived in Geelong, and later in the year, when I was still five, we moved three hours away to Wodonga. In Wodonga we moved to four different homes before I was eleven. It could be said that we were almost nomadic, moving from home to home and later from state to state. I did not question why most of our extended family lived in the same family home for years. Nor did I wonder why we kept moving; we just did.

By early adulthood, I had moved house, on average, every two years. I had been to seven different schools, both primary and high schools, and also a correspondence school. I had an average of one or two best friends at every school. The longest and most amazing school friends I have date back to when I was in grades 9 and 10 in Benalla, Victoria. I am still in contact with some of my best friends from then.

Truly, though, the only constant friends I had in childhood and my teenage years were my siblings, whom I didn't appreciate at the time. Together we faced the highs and lows of our childhood. They were my anchors, my friends and my role models. Of course we fought, as siblings do, but we were also establishing unbreakable bonds.

We had a large and close extended family. My mother was also the eldest of five children. After her came two brothers, and then two sisters, with about ten years between the eldest and youngest. My grandmother, a devoted wife and mother, cherished her loved ones. She had been one of thirteen siblings, and my grandfather, also a family man, was one of four. By the time my grandfather passed away, there were more great-grandchildren than grandchildren. He left behind a legacy of family.

My father was the youngest of four children, born just after his identical twin brother. Their two sisters were born before them. Two of his siblings had three or more children. One of his sisters married late in life and did not have children. My paternal grandparents did everything they could for their loved ones, also leaving a big family legacy.

We spent a lot of time with both our maternal and paternal extended families throughout my childhood. Our grandparents played a big role in our lives, and for that, I have always been thankful.

Some of the best times we had were at Christmas and celebrations for our relations. It was times like our annual Christmas Day water fight that created the happiest memories. My maternal grandparents lived at the end of a cul-de-sac. The water fight would end up out onto the footpath of the court with water flowing in every direction until we were all drenched, kids and adults alike.

I adored my maternal grandmother. I remember saying to one of my friends one day, 'I love my grandparents more than my parents!' She told me not to be silly. I certainly didn't feel silly. It wasn't as if I were raging those words at my parents in an angry voice; I was telling my friend how I felt. She had a good relationship with her parents and couldn't comprehend my words.

Sadly, apart from having the title of being my parents, they hadn't earned my love and respect as my grandparents had. Certainly, Grandparents spoil and have a different bond with their grandchildren. My grandparents held a special place in my heart, even at that stage of my life, and my parents did not. I feel a pang of sadness and even guilt to admit it, but it's how I thought at the time.

If we weren't at home, school or playing, we were at our maternal grandparents' home. They lived around the corner, and we would often just run around to their home, just because we could. Maybe we were running to them so that we could feel safe and be ourselves.

My grandmother, my siblings and I would cook ANZAC biscuits, vanilla-custard slice or jelly slice. More often than not, our help was more of a hindrance. We would lick the bowl clean and joke about the bowl not needing to be washed after we'd finished. I still have my grandmother's old Kenwood Chef mixing bowl with the information booklet it came with in 1971. Whenever I use it, I smile and remember her.

We loved doing anything for our grandmother, even the hideous task of ironing. Of course, we wouldn't iron at home. Looking back, it was having the choice to do something, rather than being told what to do. If we were asked to do something respectfully and nicely, we would. To be more precise, when our parents told us to do a task like ironing, given a choice, we would choose not to do it. Our grandmother did not ask us; we just did it.

That was until the day my sister asked our grandmother what would happen if you ironed over the ironing cord. She replied that you might electrocute yourself. Promptly, my sister chose not to iron after that.

Our backyard antics often included wheelbarrow races. It was a competitive wheelbarrow race of two or more teams, comprised of my siblings, cousins and sometimes our grandmother. The 'wheelbarrow' would kneel and place their hands on the ground, then lift their feet and legs so the 'driver' could hold onto them. The wheelbarrow and the driver would then race to the finish line, usually the fence at the end of the yard.

My grandmother, being the fun-loving person she was, wouldn't always play the driver; sometimes she would play the wheelbarrow, racing across the grass with her hands. As you can imagine, it was a fast-paced game that our grandmother enjoyed being part of. Often after the race, we would end up on the grass laughing hysterically.

As a hard-working lady, she worked as a personal assistant to the Minister for Immigration during World War II. She would be the first to see the war photos of the fallen. Hence, it was often at her discretion as to which photos the families would be given. I can't begin to imagine the toll it would have taken on her.

Later, she worked on telephone exchanges and then alongside my grandfather on their farm in country Victoria. They settled on the farm as part of the World War II Soldier Settler Scheme, which my grandfather was granted.[1] The land was allocated to returned servicemen, like my grandfather, to support primary production and boost post-war employment and the subsequent economy.

It was a hard life on the land, a life filled with dignity and respectability. They faced financial hardships. The outside issues included predators, weeds in the ground and adjusting to farm life. They were isolated from family and friends. They did, however, find their community within the small farming district.

They raised their five children there. After their children had moved out of home, they settled in Wodonga. My grandmother found work as a secretary in the Sanyo Factory. They also moved around a bit, within New South Wales and Victoria, during their lives, living many years in each home before moving to another location.

My maternal grandfather was a very humble family man and completely devoted to my grandmother. Due to his experience as a fitter and turner, he joined as an engine room artificer with the rank of Petty Officer in the Australian Navy during World War II. He was aboard HMAS Hobart when it was hit by a torpedo from a Japanese submarine. He survived; twenty others were killed or injured. I believed it affected his hearing, but I am sure the psychological scars were deep.

He played Australian Rules Football. I believe he could have been very good, but it was a time when players didn't earn enough money to support themselves or a family. To me, he was a gentle man with big hands and fingers, like the hands of an industrious man. In fun, he would often grab hold of your hand and squeeze it so tightly that your hand would begin to hurt. My grandmother used to say that he did not know his own strength.

As an adult, I would often ring Grandma to ask her how to cook something or get the stains out of a clothing item. If Grandpa answered the phone, once he realised it was me, he would say, 'Oh, you want to talk to Grandma.' He'd often be in the background, just doing his own thing.

I was devastated when my grandma passed away in 1996, a year before my first child was born. But for my grandpa, it meant that he was no longer in the background. As much as I missed her terribly, I am thankful that I had the next decade or so to get to know the little things about him. Things like how he used to sleep with his football as a child. When I visited, we'd walk around his garden as he showed me whatever he had growing at the time. As an avid lawn bowler, he played for his club in the pennant league. His fence adjoined the bowling club, giving him his own private access.

It appeared that he sank into a depression with his world gone when my grandmother passed away. Then, sometime later, another lady came into his life. Their marriage gave him a new lease of life as they travelled and lived their lives together. Because of this, we had many more years with him before he passed away. I am thankful to his second wife for that.

We didn't live as close to my paternal grandparents. Sadly, I did not spend as much time with them. But the times we did spend with them were amazing.

My grandfather, also a war veteran, served as a gunner in World War I, specifically in France with the Artillery Brigade, a heavy artillery unit. He was involved in the operation, maintenance and use of heavy weapons.

As a child he seemed so tall, to me, at five foot eight. He was taller than I am, but my two sons are taller than he was.

He always sat at the end of the table, reading the newspaper. I remember him often showing me his vintage duck cigarette dispenser, which sat on the mantle shelf. The duck's beak would mechanically move downwards to retrieve a cigarette. I was always fascinated by the duck and enjoyed watching him show me how it worked.

My grandfather was a very skilled and handy carpenter building many homes in the Geelong area. He and his wife, my nanna, or as we called her, Marsie, lived in their home pretty much all their married life, until he passed away when I was seven. Marsie continued to live there until she was 98, at which time she moved in with her daughter, my aunt, for the extra care that she needed. She passed away six weeks before her 101st birthday. I didn't attend her 100th birthday celebration due to distance and being very pregnant. My son was born 16 days later.

Their home had an outhouse toilet and laundry. Marsie hand-washed her clothes, and then she would use the now-vintage wringer to wring the water out. She would turn the handle, guiding each item of clothing to move through twin rollers. I was about ten years old when she finally got a modern automatic washing machine. She didn't have to manually wash her clothes anymore. A modern indoor toilet was also installed in the bathroom in the main part of the house.

Her bed seemed so big to me as a child. When any of us kids stayed there overnight, we would go and jump into bed with her in the morning. It was an awesome and fun way to start our day.

Marsie loved to cook or bake. Her stove was an old wood-burning cast-iron stove and oven. For many years, she had a family gathering at her home once a week for morning tea. I remember her baking her coconut jam drops in that wood oven. They were so yummy and melted in your mouth.

I followed her tradition of such gatherings with our—mine and Angus's—blended family of five children after my eldest son moved out. For all seven of us, and their partners, we have dinner at home every second Sunday night. I am sure that at the time, Marsie did not realise that she was creating a tradition that I would follow years later.

Marsie didn't learn to drive. I remember her walking to her church or walking up to the main shopping area. She was a deacon in their local Baptist Church. She was very respectful, and I am sure the church community showed her respect as well. Most families of the day had a high regard for honour and respectability.

While my father's family was respectable and very church-oriented, I did not see that, or it wasn't pushed onto us as children in the same way as previous generations. I am more aware of how my mother's family appeared to govern their lives around going to church on Sunday. I'm not sure why I noticed that.

My childhood with my siblings and parents was pretty mundane on the surface. Like many families from the 1970s and 1980s, we were only allowed to speak when spoken to. Today, that would be seen as rude, demeaning and controlling. When we raised our children, we taught them to have a voice, to have confidence and to be who they are. We were certainly not allowed to have or be any of that when growing up.

The fun we had was mostly with our extended family. During the summertime, we would get together with my dad's twin brother, his wife and their five children. It has always fascinated me that they had the opposite sibling arrangement to us: four boys, and the only girl was the second eldest.

My dad, who wasn't a car enthusiast, drove a white Holden HQ station wagon with a front bench seat. The retractable seat belts of today are quite different to the rigid seat belts us kids tried to use when sitting in the backseat. Today, my father would be fined for not securing the backseat passengers in their own seatbelts.

The sole positive aspect of the car not having air-conditioning was that the windows remained open while driving. That meant that the cigarette smoke would mostly go out the window when my parents smoked with us in the car.

My dad's identical twin brother also had a similar car to my dad's, but his car was a tan colour. He would have most of his five children in the back seat of the car. Our fathers would drive us to the beach on a warm, sunny summer day. I don't remember building sandcastles or even swimming in the water, but I am sure we did.

In Winter, our relatives from each side would drive to the Snowy Mountains, often Mount Buller, in convoy. We would throw snowballs at each other's heads and bodies. Tobogganing with cardboard boxes or hessian bags brought from home was also a fun part of playing in the snow.

My parents would hire a large bus and organise their own winery tour in the local region, with relatives and close friends. During the bus rides, my dad would often instigate a sing-along—with a deep singing voice, he may have thought he had a good singing voice. That is all that I remember from those winery tours.

It sounds like all we did was go to wineries, the beach in Summer and the snow in Winter. But those were just the times we spent with extended family. I am thankful for those memories now; they showed us a true indication of what family was all about.

The five of us kids fought a lot when we were young. I am told that at the age of four, I tried to wipe out three of my siblings. I had them all in a line, and I was ready to swipe them with a four-by-four plank of wood when my mother caught me. As a four-year-old, I didn't have the strength to achieve my plan, and of course, I didn't understand the gravity of how this situation may have unfolded. Thankfully, my mother stopped me in my tracks.

Despite our struggles and fights at home, we were always there for each other. If another child were treating one of our siblings poorly with words or fists, one of us would be there to prevent that. The school grapevine worked very well.

Our parents were seemingly ordinary people, living what seemed to be ordinary, typical lives. Well, at least it must have looked this way from the outside. However, did our parents truly adhere to society's standard for the domestic way of life? Or were they unconsciously playing the game?

It would have been financially hard to raise five children. Even with both of them working, it would have been difficult to make ends meet. To change their financial situation, my parents decided to work together in their own businesses. The first one, in Victoria, was a small milk bar that sold newspapers and magazines, one or two-cent lollies and ice creams. At the back of the shop was a sandwich bar that sold sandwiches, rolls and hot pies. They had the lunch contracts for two of the local factories. My father would deliver the lunches in the back of his little white van.

The second business they owned and ran was in Queensland. They chose this business because it fuelled my father's wish to do more than make and sell sandwiches and hot pies. A fish-and-chip shop run during business hours in an industrial area was the ideal business for him. My father would deliver the lunches to the workers while riding my brother's BMX bike with an Esky attached to the front handlebars. Quite a sight at times, I would imagine.

My father was not a good boss. Quite often, he wouldn't pay the five of us when we worked in either shop. His employees in the fish-and-chip shop put up with his flirtatious ways. That was not right and would not be tolerated today.

My father had many other jobs in his working life. He did not have a trade or a qualification, although I believe he may have posed as a carpenter, though he was not. He did renovate a few homes over the years. He worked as a labourer or a station hand and in insurance before I was born. The jobs I remember him doing were working as a bartender at the local SS&A club and in the factory for Uncle Ben's dog food.

In his day, he may have been a 'catch'. He wasn't a tall man, probably about the same height as his father but he had dark curly hair and an often-cheeky grin. He maintained a slim waistline to the point that it was almost an obsession. He was probably a completely different man from the beau my mother would have known, in part due to his larrikinisms. He lived in the moment, not in the past nor the future. That would be evident throughout my parents' relationship.

In the same context, my mother was someone entirely different to those my father had previously been interested in or captivated by. I believe their attraction was almost instant when they met while she was a student at teachers' college in Geelong. From her graduation photo, she had poise—a quiet presence. She looked stunning with her head held high and her hair in a beautiful French braid.

After teachers' college, my mother taught in primary school and later as a preschool teacher. We knew that she had a beautiful operatic voice in her days at teachers' college. After working as a preschool teacher, singing nursery rhymes to the children, my mother was unable to use the operatic part of her voice. Later, when my parents' second business was sold, my mother decided that it was time for her to retire, and my father worked as a cleaner at the local TAFE.

What my mother did not know when they met was that my father was a divorcee and the father of three daughters, one deceased. It was the 1960s. During that era, there was an expectation that one would start a perfect family. Divorce and children from a previous marriage were taboo and would bring shame and disgrace. That was not okay.

My father would bring shame to my mother's family, and she had no idea.

My father was introduced to my mother's parents in an unpretentious affair. When meeting most people, my grandfather was a good judge of character. He would have been even more on guard since he was meeting a possible suitor for his eldest daughter.

It was a normal day in late 1965 or early 1966. The atmosphere was courteous but quiet. At the time, my grandparents still lived on their farm in country Victoria.

The 1960s were tumultuous and sometimes divisive. This included the birth of the civil rights movement, advancement towards workplace equality for women, and the beginnings of legal recognition for Aboriginal and Torres Strait Islander Peoples. The Beatles were a phenomenon, pickleball had been invented, and Star Trek, Batman and The Grinch made their screen debuts. A litre of milk was nineteen cents; a litre of petrol was seven cents; and the FJ Holden was valued at $2,200. With an average income per week of $60, the price of a home averaged $4,400.

I believe the conversation would have started something like this when my father greeted his future in-laws.

'Hello, Mr and Mrs Stevens, it's nice to meet you,' my father would have said with a cheeky grin on his face.

'Well, that remains to be seen, doesn't it, son?' my grandfather would have retorted a little too quickly.

As previously stated, my father did not allude to his previous marriage and the children born from this relationship, but he also did not let them know he was thirteen years older than my mother.

His rugged, boyish looks gave the perception that he was younger—much younger.

He held these truths from my mother and her parents for a few years. Despite all of that, as my grandparents got to know him, they did love him as their daughter's partner.

But more was yet to come.

Both of my grandparents were upstanding members of their community and church. To them, family gave dignity and respectability. My parents tried to maintain that sense of decency and dignity. Despite appearances, we were far from perfect, and often far from dignified or respectable at times.

When dining out today, children often use iPads or phones for entertainment. Interaction is sometimes limited. When we were children, our interaction was also minimal. We didn't have anything to entertain us. We would sit at the table, not talking, just eating what was in front of us. Despite our likes or dislikes, we would have to eat all of the food, the meat and three vegetables or my mum's favourite, tuna mornay.

Our mother was often harsh. On one occasion, we were having chops for dinner. We weren't allowed to pick up the chops and use our fingers to finish the meat on the bone until we asked her in the way she deemed to be right. Time seemed to drag on, asking if we could pick up the chops in every manner you could think of. I think we did ask correctly from the beginning, but she wouldn't let us pick up the chops. One of my sisters even put the chop in the bin, and our mother made her get it out.

I think it was then that I told her that I would be a vegetarian when I grew up, and she told me not to be ridiculous. At eighteen I became a vegetarian, and I still am. My father did not accept me being a vegetarian. He would try to encourage me to have a steak at every opportunity.

I started to misbehave well before I was in grade six. But I do remember being caught having my first cigarette with friends as we hid in the adventure playground of the school grounds at that age. Of course, my parents were promptly notified. I was one of the lucky ones. My friends were all punished by being banned from doing certain things and other reprimands. My father said to me, 'Don't do it again.'

Years later, I asked him why my punishment was not harsher. He said, 'I could hardly tell you not to smoke when I smoked.'

Money was scarce in our household. My clothes were daggy and often second-hand before being handed down to my siblings. The clothes would be re-worn from weekend to weekend. Even in the cold Victorian winter, I often wore a short pink skirt when inside because I did not have enough long pants or warmer clothes to wear. One cold winter day, while wearing that skirt and serving customers behind the counter in our milkbar shop, some girls from school walked past. There was nowhere to hide; they could see me through the big glass window at the shop's front. I heard them laughing and saying, 'She's wearing a skirt!'

Our parents ensured that we played sports. The girls played netball, David played Australian Rules Football, and we all did Little Athletics. Our mum was the secretary of the Little Athletics club. Mum would take us to community activities like the local Christmas carols. This all helped maintain the sense of family respectability and honourability.

Each week, Jennifer, Cynthia and I would walk a few kilometres to our netball games, just the three of us, no adults. On one occasion, dressed in our netball uniforms, we knocked on the door of someone's home.

'We are raising money for the netball association; would you like to donate?' We lied. We didn't have any tickets or forms to sign as proof that we were raising money for our club, but they must have felt pity for us, and they gave us a handful of loose coins. We had enough money to buy some snacks from the tuckshop at the netball courts. Telling our parents would bring dishonour, so we kept that to ourselves for many years.

Our brother, David, as the boy in the family, was always treated like the special one. He'd get in trouble less frequently, have fewer chores to do around the house, and be given more attention. I did not understand why that was that way until many years later.

Regardless of the reason, I couldn't help being a little jealous when both of our parents would drive to his football games each week. In hindsight, the games were not usually, though not always, within walking distance of home. But going to his football games as a family was something else that maintained the appearance of respectability. Our netball games did not register as far as that was concerned.

Though our parents and often our maternal grandparents would come to our netball end-of-year games if our teams made the finals. My father and grandfather would be barracking or yelling instructions to me or our team members from the sidelines. When the umpire asked them to stop, their sense of humour would often show by barracking for the other team, hoping that the other team would be penalised.

We enjoyed swimming at the local pool. It was another thing that we did without parental supervision. The twins and I would be dropped off by ourselves, often for hours. Then we would walk home, about a kilometre, by ourselves. For three young girls, around ten years old, it would have taken us around 20 minutes, provided we walked at a normal pace.

After swimming for hours, we were often hungry. On one occasion, we had no money, no food, and a long, impending walk ahead. Instead of walking straight home, we turned and walked an extra half kilometre in the other direction to the local supermarket. Jennifer and I went in. One of us put a block of chocolate in one of our bags for some sustenance for the walk home. Though the chocolate would have boosted our stamina, it would not have filled our hungry bellies.

After we left the supermarket and started walking home, Cynthia said that she wasn't having any part of it. She wasn't going to eat any of the chocolate, but we knew that if she had some, she could not tell Mum and Dad. Somehow, we talked her into it. I guess she must have been just as hungry as we were.

Although on these occasions we tricked our way into getting money for food, or took what wasn't ours without paying, we were hungry. We did get fed at home, but only what we were given. Five children during those times took a lot to feed, clothe, school and house. Our household, for various reasons, not just this, was a challenging environment. Not that I am making any excuses nor advocating any of it. I am grateful for what we had.

At that time, we lived in what we called an upside-down boat house, across the road from a playground. We spent a lot of fun times together, just the five of us, or some of our cousins, in that park, especially during the summer heat. The parkland, adjacent to our side of the road, was bordered by a steep hill. We would often roll down the hill over and over again, from the top to the bottom. Then, when we had had enough of that, we would run through the creek that ran behind the parkland to cool down. Often, a leech would attach to our legs. We would grab them off with our hands and throw them back into the creek. Pretty gross when I think about it now.

Hours would go by with us rarely seeing another soul, including our parents or any adults. After having fun and amusing ourselves, we would dawdle with heavy feet all the way home. Sleep would always come easily on those nights.

The house we lived in before the upside-down house was number six. Because I was six years old at the time, it became my favourite number. Later in life, it would become my least favourite number, as many loved ones passed away with the number six in the date, month or year of their passing.

That house also had a playground very close by—two houses away from us. At some point, I had gone into the playground alone to teach myself how to swing without the assistance of someone else. I learnt to swing my legs harder and harder to go higher and higher. I was achieving my goal, then all of a sudden, I felt unwell. I vomited all over myself. Even though I washed myself down, I would have still smelled of vomit. I am unsure if my parents noticed. From then on, I suffered from motion sickness.

My mindset of 'children are seen and not heard' was amplified in our house. To me, it was like a type of hierarchy, where you could not talk to parents or adults. Unless we were spoken to first, we did not initiate conversation.

Extended family members have referred to the five of us kids by saying that we raised ourselves. Unless we did something wrong, the guidance was lacking for us children. We did not understand or know why. Nor did we comprehend or understand our mother's distance towards us. She was not maternal and showed little affection. If we fell over from running too fast or from riding our shared bike, or just from hurting ourselves in the park or yard, I do not remember our mother picking us up and cuddling us.

My brother David, though, remained the favourite one. At a recent loved one's funeral, it was told to my sister that my mum would push any of us girls to the side if my brother headed towards her so he could sit on her lap. I do not remember this. I hope that even at that young age, I did not take this to heart. Knowing myself and my sisters, we probably did. Little did we know that there may have been a reason for this.

If we wanted any attention, we would have to step outside the box and do something good. I won a colouring competition at school, I would tell a joke, or I'd get sporting merit at different times. But at what cost?

To reiterate, when I was thirteen, my father decided to move us yet again. This time we moved to a different town, the third town I had lived in. My parents decided to purchase a little milk bar in Benalla. They opened the doors seventeen hours a day, thankfully, with the residence behind the business.

Having easy access to junk food with the shop—lollies, chocolates, milkshakes and ice creams—and early teenage hormonal changes, we all gained weight. Our father did not like our weight gain.

Our lifelong bonds grew stronger during these teen years as we began forming our own identities. Unfortunately, without supervision, somewhat due to our parents working in the shop all day, every day, we did not always make the best decisions, and we often found ourselves in trouble.

We got up on the roof of the shop on one occasion and smoked a packet of cigarettes. I didn't even know how to draw back on a cigarette. Thankfully, I did not take it up as an adult.

For whatever reason, we decided to steal from the local newsagency. This time, we got caught by the shop owner. Our parents were their customers, purchasing the local papers and magazines for the milk bar.

'What are we going to do?' one of us asked when we regrouped after.

'I guess we will have to own up to it. We have to get back to the shop before the newsagent owners tell Mum and Dad.'

We knew what we had done was wrong. Pity that didn't stop us from doing it. The fear of the ramifications set in, and so, we waited until dark before going home. We thought that with a bit of luck, Dad would be in a better mood by then. Our plan did not work. He was furious, and he made us go back to the shop the next day and apologise. I vaguely remember returning the items to the owner. It was a hard lesson looking back, but necessary.

I also got into trouble with some of my school friends. Often we would have to report to the school principal. Somehow, I discovered that the principal was a cousin of my maternal grandfather. I mentioned that to him, hoping for some undeserved leniency, while I sat opposite him in his office. He responded by saying that many students in the school could be related to him. Clemency and tolerance were not part of his vocabulary that day. It should not have been either. I vaguely remember having to pick up papers on the school oval as my punishment.

I had my first and only school wagging issue with a friend. We went into the main area of the town and walked around. It was so stressful, and then we were seen by one of the teachers. We were so worried that the teacher would report us that we went back to school after the bell. The teacher did not report us. At our next class, no one had even noticed that we were gone. The anxiety was so intense that I did not wag school again.

I had my first kiss behind the town's civic centre building. Why there, I do not know. I wouldn't even call it a kiss. It was over before it had even begun. Surprising to no one, including myself, we didn't become boyfriend and girlfriend after our amazing peck.

I had my first experiences with alcohol in the car park when a group of my friends went to the Blue Light Disco. It's possible I swigged one mouthful of alcohol, a bit like my first kiss was just a peck, not a full-on pash. Either that or I danced away the effects of the alcohol as my parents didn't notice. Whatever the effect, we were merely experimenting.

I am still good friends with some of these ladies. They are amazing people who are family-oriented, with their own families and grandchildren. I'm truly grateful to call them my friends.

With a different group of friends, there were other incidents that I deeply regret now. We did not do anything to harm another person, but we could have faced real consequences. I own my culpability in that. But we were influenced by our environment and some of our peers. I was banned from hanging out with one of those friends by my parents when they deemed her a bad influence.

Looking back, I can see how easily, especially without parental supervision, this type of behaviour can happen. Our lack of parental supervision is not an excuse, but it certainly did contribute.

However, I do think that our parents must have known more than I remember because our dad sold the shop and we moved once again. Ironically, a local police officer bought the shop for his wife to run.

We had lived there for two years. By the end of the school year, we had left. Mum and Dad had bought a 20-foot caravan to sleep us all. With the money they made from the sale of the shop, we would travel the South-East coast of Australia over the next eight months. Travelling like that was not as common or popular then as it is today.

My parents did not know how to save and keep money for a rainy day. They would preach to us to save our money in case we needed it one day, but they did not do that themselves. It was as if money would burn a hole in their pockets. Granted, a life on the road with five teenagers and no income for months would not have been cheap.

While travelling, the five of us continued our education by correspondence school, the toughest schooling I ever had. It was so hard to understand and comprehend what we were meant to do from the workbooks. I think I failed maths. Our mum was meant to help, but either she did not know how or she did not want to help.

Eight months and several thousand kilometres later, my father pulled the van into a caravan park in Palm Beach, Queensland. We stayed there for a couple of months. From there, my parents looked for our next home. It was an outer suburb of Brisbane that would become home for the next few years.

I left a lot of my bad habits and even worse actions behind. Starting a new school in the last two years of my schooling proved hard too. I found friends, not an easy thing to do when you are the newcomer in the last two years of high school. I began noticing myself—what I did, my behaviour and my thinking patterns. I became more of an introvert. This school was the seventh school I attended.

Not only was I trying to find my way, but my confused teenage self had too much responsibility placed on my shoulders by my parents. My parents bought the second business, a fish-and-chip shop in an industrial area. It did not have the residence behind the shop, like the corner milk bar. So, my parents would have been gone before we all got out of bed, and they wouldn't be there when we got home from school. The five of us kids walked to school every day—rain, hail or shine. One particular day, the school called our parents because we were drenched to the core. My dad came to pick us up to take us home to change. The only thing I had to wear back to school was an old netball skirt—pretty embarrassing for a grade eleven student.

Apart from the embarrassment of situations like that one, I also had my mindset to contend with. Little did I know then that I had a 'monkey mind', and as such, I was my own worst critic, tangled in self-criticism and self-doubt, leaving me uncertain and unkind to myself. I treated my friends with kindness and understanding, but I didn't know how to offer the same compassion to myself.

What made it worse was the hideous nickname of 'Bull' that clung to me, shaping how I saw myself for years. When anyone addressed me using that name, I would cringe for two reasons. The first reason was that I had the most awful cowlick, or a double crown. That is when your hair grows to a point on the scalp and forms a circular formation. It can also be known as a whorl. When you have two whorls, it is called a double crown.

'Having a double crown of hair on your head has been associated with many myths, such as balding, being intelligent, or being autistic. However, no research supports this.'[2] I certainly could not relate to any of those myths. It gave me a hideous look that I was ashamed of. We were not able to use hair products, and so I could not soften the blow. What it meant to me was that I had an ugly fringe area, resembling bull horns, that I detested. It could have been worse, but as a teenager, I was not aware of that.

At the hairdresser's one day, the lady cutting my hair asked me if I used conditioner in my hair. I replied, 'No, we only use conditioner when we go to the hairdresser.' I'm sure my mother would have been so embarrassed by my response. But I also knew that conditioner may not have helped; I needed a mountain of hair products to make that hairstyle look good.

The second reason I gained my nickname was the fact that I roared or yelled like a bull. You see, I was often 'put in charge' of my siblings when my parents weren't home. As a teen, trying to find my feet in life and dealing with siblings like a parent should, I would yell at them. They did not deserve that either. I think we all faced internal struggles.

Sometimes this role was given to one of my siblings as a reward or to punish me. It was times like these that I longed for an elder sibling. I envied my friends who had siblings older than them. If I had an older sibling, they might have taken some of the load, maybe protected me or been a friend to me. I would often lie awake wishing for that older sibling.

During those times, I sensed my siblings, my parents and extended family did not like me. I did not like myself. As a result, I was nervous and fearful—I felt unseen and overlooked. I sensed judgment from loved ones, my classmates and teachers. Classmates would pick me last, and so I assumed I had nothing to offer.

I thought I was an 'ugly duckling', and so I would blend into the crowd or hide in the background. I was shy and softly spoken. The inner child in me suffered, and I ignored the fun and the joy in doing things that would make me shine. I didn't think that anyone, including myself, knew the real me. I didn't allow myself to be my true self. Looking back at myself, it's like I am looking at someone else. I had a constant scowl on my face. It was part of the image I portrayed to others—it wasn't the type of person I wanted to be. It took me a long time to realise that and even longer to regain or reshape the image of me, for others and most importantly, for myself.

The biggest problem was that our parents did not see us. They judged us and categorised us unfairly. Our extended family did see us, but they could not prevent anything; they were not strong enough to stand up to our father.

Then, during the last two years of my schooling, I developed migraines. At first, we did not know what they were—no one else suffered with blurred vision, like ripples running through my eyeballs, pounding headaches, numbness and sometimes vomiting. Like other things when we were growing up, our parents thought we did it for the attention. Possibly at times that was true, but a migraine cannot be faked.

It was amazing to find out the name for what was happening to me. I'd been suffering from migraines due to the stress of completing senior school and our home life. A lot of the stress came from my father, who showed me his true colours during this time—some parts of which I am not ready to write about.

I will write about one particular day when whatever belief I had left in my parents, in particular my father, was shattered further. We were all in the backyard playing cricket. I had been bowled out on the first ball that I faced. Before this day, if you went out on the first ball, you were always given another chance.

On this day, that ruling did not apply. I argued the point that it's not fair to go out on the first ball, but my challenge fell on deaf ears. In my moment of rage, I picked up one of the plastic chairs and threw it. Then I stormed off upstairs.

Cynthia turned to everyone and said, 'Look what you've done now.'

We lived in an old Queenslander house that my father purchased to renovate. He followed me into the house and met me as I was about to go out the front door.

'Stop!' He called out.

Where was I going, anyway? I do not know.

Hearing him, I stopped and turned to face him. The front door was behind me as I pleaded my case. I was saying how unfair it was. I thought he was there to help, to listen or to coax me back to continue the game.

But instead, he reached towards me as if he was going to slap or push me. His hand connected, and somehow my head flung backwards and ended up in the small leadlight glass window at the top of the front door. My head vibrated off the window. The glass cracked like a ripple in a lake of water. Some strands of my hair got stuck in the crack of the glass. Instead of replacing the glass, my father patched it with cardboard, plastic and tape, with a few strands of my hair still attached; a constant reminder of what happened.

Afterwards, I was in shock. I don't even know if I yelled or screamed, or if I just turned and ran out the front door, down the stairs and into the street. My sisters went looking for me around our home. I think I came home about a few hours later, after my tears had dried.

Around the same time, I took Jennifer and Cynthia to a party. The two ladies who worked for my parents in their takeway shop somehow invited us, as either guests themselves or the hosts. I was driving by that stage. My mother was having drinks in the lounge room. My other siblings—David, Nancy and Lee, our half-sister from our dad's first marriage, and her son—were playing Uno. Every time they banged their hand on the table to say Uno, my mother freaked out, thinking the police were knocking on the front door, coming to tell her that the three of us had been killed in a car accident.

I think it was around this time that the ladies from the shop no longer worked for our parents in the shop. I do not recall why or if it had anything to do with the party.

Nonetheless, we didn't have an accident; I just brought my sisters home later than my parents thought. When we got home an argument followed. One of my siblings told me that somehow my father ended up on my back, and two of my siblings were trying to pull him off me.

It was not long after that the five of us all ran away to our Aunty Lisa, our mum's sister's, home. Lee and her son were still staying with us at the time; they came with us. She had a rocky relationship with our father; he would often refer to her as 'Driftwood.'

We stayed there for a couple of days. At that point, in a bid for reconciliation, my aunt talked to our parents and convinced them to come to her home and talk with us about it.

Instead of a normal greeting, when my father saw us all, he said, 'F**k you all!'

We would have been within our rights to walk away at that point. But our father was not a man you messed with. Eventually, the comment was followed by productive discussion. Some of us did go home, and Lee and her son went back to Geelong.

I do not know if our family life ever regained a true sense of normalcy, whatever that was.

Life as a family unit had certainly started to change. Before then, we had our issues; we hid a lot from those outside the walls of our home. I learnt to put on a blank face so no one would know how I felt. Well, at least that is what I thought.

Some of our extended family knew little bits. Ultimately, my relationship with my parents was not what it should have been. It was not like the relationship that my friends had with their parents. I did not realise just how much I wanted a close mother-daughter relationship until I had my own daughter.

And so began the next phase of life when we started to move out of home. I moved in with my partner, his parents and younger sister, Jennifer joined the forces, and Cynthia moved in with her partner. Soon after, David moved to Geelong and lived with Lee and her partner for a while. Nancy was the only one left at home for some time, but as soon as she could, she also moved out. I knew that I wanted to begin my life and be free from the stress, control and everything that came with that, and I think my siblings wanted the same.

After the five of us had all left to begin our own lives, my parents moved another three times to three different suburbs. I did not know why my father moved us to so many different houses. Luckily, we were very minimalistic—our possessions were limited. I think the kitchen was the most difficult room to pack up and move.

I asked my mother why we moved around a lot. She told me that it was because my father renovated the homes. There were only three homes that I remember him renovating. I knew that was just another excuse.

Was the real reason financial? Did he like the nomadic lifestyle and could not stay put? Or was he running from something or someone?

Chapter 2

TRUTH WITHHELD

Dysfunctional families can't give you love
because love can't come from people who don't love
themselves in the first place. —Anonymous

Come as something beginning with the first letter of your name, the invite said.

It was Nancy's fortieth birthday celebration. You would think that I would be able to recall without a doubt what I wore that night, but I don't. The events of the night overshadowed everything else. It was a night that would prove to be different to any other family celebration. After that evening, everything changed.

The party was being held at Cynthia's house, where she lived with her husband Billie and their two teenage children, about an hour from our home. Being on acreage, the property allowed plenty of room for us to stay overnight, so we didn't have to worry about driving after a few drinks.

Behind the home, the block sloped. The grass was mowed, showing some brown patches indicative of a lack of rain. Beside the home, the water tanks stored the trickle feed water supply; they didn't have town water. There were times when they had to buy water for the tanks because of the Queensland drought.

My sister Cynthia was always very good at decorating and designing her home. Out the back, the scene was set with party lights adorning the pergola. Cynthia had placed the chairs and tables thoughtfully and decorated the tables with beautiful, delicate ornaments adorned with fairy lights, creating a warm, inviting ambience. Further along the pergola was the fenced pool, which was off bounds for the night. Overlooking the pool and further into the property, the trees did not show the obvious effects of the drought aside from a few scattered twigs with poor growth. To the right of the pergola was a healthy, tall lemon-scented gum tree.

My partner, Angus and I, and our teenage children arrived early in case they needed help with last-minute preparations. The birthday girl, Nancy, her husband George and their teenage children had already arrived.

After greeting Nancy with a warm hug, she asked me to come into the main bedroom for a moment. I thought that she had a clothing malfunction or that she needed help with something else for the party.

When we both sat on the bed, I sensed she wanted to chat.

She seemed nervous and unsure. She flicked her head to the side and fidgeted with her fingers as she took a deep breath and said, 'I have to tell you something. Aunty Lisa rang me for my birthday.'

Nancy was referring to our mother's sister. The conversation between the two of them proved to be a chat like no other, a conversation that would change our lives forever.

'We have another sibling,' she blurted out.

'What are you talking about?' I muttered in disbelief.

'Aunty Lisa asked me a question. She asked if I was sure there were only five of us?'

That sentence would change the course of our lives. We were all forty years old and older, and we had all believed things to be a certain way for our entire lives. I was just learning that it was not true.

My interest piqued. I said, 'Say, what?'

I looked at Nancy with scepticism. She said again, 'We have another sibling!'

My mind boggled, and my heart jumped a beat.

'What do you mean?' I asked.

Nancy said, 'Aunty Lisa said that there may be another full-blooded sibling of ours who is older than you ... Mum and Dad had another child.'

I thought, no, this isn't correct. I am the eldest; I have always been the eldest. How does something like this happen after all these years? There must be a mistake; she must be misguided. Surely, it had to be wrong. I gazed out the window. Was this true? If so, how does this even happen? It was a huge piece of our family history that we knew nothing about until now. How can secrets like that be kept for generations without being known? I couldn't comprehend what I was hearing.

Nancy was telling me that, for the past forty-four years of my life and the past forty years of her life, we had been lied to. Important, huge parts of our heritage, the truth, had been withheld by our parents for all these years.

I think if I were not already sitting on the bed, I would have stumbled, much like the stammered words that came from my mouth.

'Do you mean Mum and Dad had another child before me?' I asked.

'Yes,' she replied.

Really, what would that mean? I couldn't believe what I was hearing. It had to be a ridiculous notion that had been blown out of proportion, or maybe the lies belonged to someone else's family. Maybe my aunt was muddled. I was clinging to something—what I don't know.

'Do you believe what Aunty Lisa told you?' I asked her.

'Yes, I think she was telling the truth.'

'Oh, my goodness, I have no words ...'

This was the kind of thing that you hear about in the movies, or in other people's families, but not in our family. My heart raced, my hearing muffled, like I was in a trance. I glared straight out the window, like the answer—whether it was true or not—would miraculously appear before me somehow.

I flashed back to the feelings from the past when I would be lying in bed, upset about being the 'one in charge of my siblings' and wishing that I wasn't the eldest sibling. Now, if Aunty Lisa was telling us the truth, I couldn't be the eldest! Someone else, whom we did not know, was.

What the f**k!

My sister and I exchanged glances, and I said, 'How do you feel about this information?'

'I'm not sure. I am as shocked as you are,' she replied.

We both sat for a moment or two, neither of us knowing what to say. I felt numb, confused and even frustrated. Why now?

'Do you think that what she is saying is true?' I asked, still questioning what she told me.

'Aunty Lisa believes so,' she replied.

'Why now?' I said, more as a statement than a question.

Later, I learnt that our grandfather had confided in our Aunty twenty years earlier after our grandmother passed away. He wanted us to be told one year after his passing. He left this world, and his funeral took place exactly one year prior on Nancy's birthday. Not a great day to have a funeral. I wasn't about to let something else, in this case something that we did not know to be true yet, tarnish my sister's birthday again. I knew that we would find out in good time, but it was Nancy's birthday celebration, and not a time to dwell on what we did not know for sure yet.

'Well, tonight is your celebration, we have to forget about that for now and enjoy this night for you, Nancy. Guests will be arriving soon.' I guess I was saying this just as much for her as myself. I wanted to be able to celebrate her birthday.

Other family members would also hear about it that night. But for the moment, we all had to put it aside. We hadn't known about it for over forty years; it could wait a bit longer.

Nancy and I walked out of the bedroom and onto the pergola. The party lights had been turned on. Nancy went over to the music system and turned the sound up. We needed some music to lighten the mood, to change our mindset, to get us in the mood to celebrate.

The rest of the night was filled with laughter, a few drinks or more and a delicious M&M birthday cake made by one of Cynthia's friends. I have to admit, despite the news that could have derailed the evening, it was an impressive night filled with good times together with family and Nancy's friends. The evening finished around midnight or so.

All evening, I tried to put the news to the back of my mind. But it did not leave me. At that stage of my life, the hideous nickname of Bull had been forgotten. We had all grown up, living our own lives. My siblings and I became the true friends that we were always meant to be. We would celebrate every milestone in each other's lives. We were always there if one or more of us needed a chat or a helping hand. What followed for us as siblings was another time in our lives when we would become closer. This time, it was the journey for the truth.

The following morning, the sun rose just like any other day, except it was not like any other day. The morning before the party, I had a clear mind, my world was normal and unchanged.

On the morning after the party, everything was different, although we did not talk about it. I guess we just knew life had altered.

One by one, we all got up, all quite bleary-eyed. We were all surprisingly okay, with no headaches or hangovers. Remnants of beer cans, bottles and the odd paper plate remained as a reminder of a great night. We cleaned all of that up before my brothers-in-law Billie and George made a hearty breakfast of bacon and eggs on muffins on the BBQ.

The chatter was limited that morning. No one mentioned what had been talked about the previous night. It was as if the conversation had not happened. Maybe if we didn't bring it up, our lives wouldn't transform. I'm sure we weren't ready to come to grips with the lies or the truths withheld until now. No plans were made.

After breakfast, we all packed up our things. One by one, we all said bye and headed back to our own homes. It would be there that we could find the time and solace to make sense of the information we had just learnt about our family.

Chapter 3
HOW DARE YOU?

Knowing is not enough; we must apply. Willing is not enough; we must do. —Johann Wolfgang von Goethe[3]

Back at home, we went about our usual Sunday; the typically energetic and humming household of two adults and five teenagers—Angus and my blended family. We set about doing things like ensuring we had uniforms for school and work the next day, tidying the house and making dinner. I found it tough to focus on the tasks I had to do.

It was not until the quiet of the evening, when the teens had gone to bed, that I lay in my bed and let my mind drift. I allowed myself to wonder what this meant and how it would change everything. I was trying to understand and comprehend it all. But really, I didn't know what to feel, what to think and truthfully, what to do. All I could feel was numbness, like an envelope encapsulating me in a bubble of questions. Only I couldn't answer the questions.

What surprised me then were the tears that started to spill down my cheeks. If I'm truthful, in my later teenage years, I hid my emotions so tightly that I hardly ever cried. Even in my adulthood, I didn't cry. It had only been in the last year that I'd felt more alive than ever, and with that came emotions, tears and, of course, happiness. I would cry for myself, but also for others, and sometimes over silly things, like scenes in movies.

In that moment, I knew that I needed to feel the grief, the sorrow, the complete and utter rejection. We were kept in the dark. It is possible we were not meant to know at all.

I had so many questions when I thought about my parents, and it began to consume me. They'd held the truth from us. How and why could this happen?

We had been lied to for over four decades. Did I have a right to feel that way? How was I going to deal with this? I did not know.

At the time, I was experiencing grief and sadness for what had been taken from us without our knowledge. We had the older sibling that I had longed for. That person could be out there. How dare that knowledge be taken from us!

There must be more to this. There must be a valid reason, but what? I was not ready to be empathetic and understanding towards my parents. I was appalled that they'd kept us in the dark. Lying in my bed in the dark of my room, it was easier to feel sorry for myself and my siblings. Everything about our family that we thought was true was no longer.

We were not children; we could have accepted this knowledge had we been told earlier. It felt like they did not trust us. They had betrayed us and made choices by unjustly withholding the truth. The sense of that made what I was feeling worse, much worse.

That Sunday evening in my bed, I felt overwhelmed by the anger and the pain that comes from deep heartache and sorrow. I sensed myself disconnecting. How could I deal with such strong emotions? Looking back, I can see that I was heading towards the five stages of grief, beginning with denial. Was it real or just a vivid dream? Was it made up? Where were the facts to prove the truth beyond a doubt?

How could the five of us deal with the lies and deception? Even when we were growing up, the sheer number of us seemed abnormal. Most of our school friends' families had two or three children. We had five. Now we were even more abnormal, with another sibling.

Our new sibling had spent their life without their siblings. They wouldn't have known that they came from a big biological family. All of a sudden, we had become the relatives with secrets, with lies, and so many unanswered questions.

I wondered whether my sibling was still alive, and if so, where did they live? Were they happy? Were they married, or had they been married, with children of their own? What did they do for a job, a career?

Without knowing it, had any of us walked past them in the street and not noticed the resemblance? Did they look or talk like us? Perhaps, they were not like us at all.

If our sibling had been raised with us, would I have had a good relationship with them? Would I have liked them and they me? Would my parents have had the rest of us if this sibling had been raised with us? Of course, I didn't know any of this yet.

At the time, I couldn't put it into words or understand it. My heart was breaking. I felt pain in my chest, and my breath became short. I ached, but somehow, I drifted off to sleep.

I woke again at 2:00 am. The questions in my mind raced once more. The anger welled up, and I needed to get back to sleep before work the next day. I worked as a nurse in primary care. I really needed to sleep.

I decided that the best way to rest my mind would be to get some sleep and call my Aunty Lisa as soon as I could. I needed to hear her words with my own ears. It was time to find out if this secret was true. I could then determine if my anger was justified or not.

Aunty Lisa was younger than my mother by eight years. She had three of her own children. It was always a lot of fun when, as children, we all spent some of the school holidays at Aunty Lisa's home with her and her children. It was a happy time away from home when we could laugh and enjoy each day. We had a different relationship with her than our parents; she was more attentive.

On one occasion, after holidays with Aunty on my birthday, Cynthia and I flew home in a small twin-engine plane with about eight other people. Our flight was delayed due to flashing lightning that illuminated the night sky like fireworks. Thunder crashed, banged and roared. We sat in the airport for several hours until it was okay to fly. The turbulent flight did not ease my and Cynthia's anxiety about flying and our motion sickness. I don't remember staying with Aunty Lisa after that, probably due to logistics more than anything else.

As planned during that sleepless night, I found a few moments to call her the next evening. I'm sure she was expecting my call and answered after three rings. After we said our initial greeting, I got straight to it.

'I'm sorry, it just slipped out,' she said.

'It wasn't great timing,' I said.

I let her know I was not angry at her. It wasn't her fault that we didn't know. But I did wonder why the news had not been revealed the year before, after my grandfather passed, or even after my grandmother passed away years before.

'Why did you wait this long to tell one of us?' I asked, puzzled.

'Dad wanted it that way,' she told me, referring to my maternal grandfather.

She also told me that my grandfather speculated on the truth. He didn't know the whole story, just parts of it. She told me that he believed that the baby was a girl, born in December 1967 or January 1968.

He may have thought the baby was a girl since my dad had so many girl children: three daughters from his first marriage and four from his second. My grandfather knew about one son, my younger brother David.

As I spoke to Aunty Lisa, I could hear the emotion in her voice. She had no reason not to tell us the truth. Nor did our grandfather have any reason not to tell her the truth. Yet there were still so many questions.

During this chat, Aunty Lisa opened up about why my grandfather had wanted to wait to tell us. He had kept this secret deep within his heart for all these years. I wanted to know why.

'He was always upset when he spoke about it,' she said. 'He was concerned about the child. He used to say, "One day that child is going to come knocking on their door, and they will have to face up to their secret. My guess is they will lie and deny it."'

She paused and continued, 'Grandpa would not have lied about that; don't be scared.'

But he chose not to tell us himself. He wanted us to know after he had passed away. My grandmother also took the secret to her grave. I was at a loss as to why neither of my grandparents told us the truth themselves. I always had a good relationship with them, and I would have thought that deserved their honesty. That was another facet I had to deal with.

At the end of our conversation, Aunty Lisa asked me if we had talked to or planned to talk to our parents. I told her we had not yet spoken to them.

After I got off the phone with Aunty Lisa, tears trickled down my cheeks. I sighed and swallowed deeply as I realised that I had no control over my emotions, especially when I thought about what was meant to be and what was not. My state of mind was a rollercoaster; heavy one minute, quiet for a moment and heavy again later. Sadness, disappointment and distress entered my life—these were not foreign feelings for me, just shaped by a different reason.

Aunty sent me a message a few days later saying she had started looking for more information. She told me that she contacted the department that handled past adoptions in Melbourne.

'I just want the truth,' she wrote. 'I have put in an application requesting identifying information from the department, meaning just the first name and locality, because I want to prove Grandpa did not lie. I don't want to locate your sibling. That's not my business. I just want the truth, but it takes up to three months. I'll let you know when I hear anything.'

I replied saying that we still had not spoken to Mum and Dad, and that maybe we would talk to them the following weekend.

She continued by writing, 'Good luck, some websites allow siblings, aunts and uncles to gain access to records. I registered interest in them. Hopefully, after the initial shock, your parents will open up with information. Even if they don't want to know.'

'Thank you. I am scared because it opens a can of worms. I have been on the post-adoption support service. They have been great, thanks.'

She replied, saying she understood my fears and that maybe it was better to wait until we had more information before talking to our parents.

Whenever I would allow myself to feel into the disappointment about the fact that we hadn't been told, I would think about what we'd been denied. I did not know my siblings. It was the simple things like sharing celebrations like Christmas and birthdays that we all take for granted. I hadn't been able to give my sibling a high five, chat to them or give them a big hug. What would it feel like to do all of those things now? How would it feel to hug my sibling?

I didn't even know what colour eyes or hair he or she would have. Or what food they liked. The possibilities of what I did not know were endless, and as such, knowing the answers to some of these possibilities had been ripped from me.

I recalled an incident when I was about thirteen or fourteen; I was angry with my parents and yelled through tears and teenage hormones, 'If I am adopted and I find that out later, I will never forgive you!'

That simple comment may have caused them to feel emotional pain deep in their hearts. As children, when we are annoyed, we may say things like, 'I don't like you.' But this would have been even more raw for my parents. There was a sense of power in my words that I was unaware of. I did not know how close I was to the truth.

I replayed my conversation with Aunty Lisa over and over again. After reflecting on our chat and the person my grandfather was, I could not deny that it was most likely true.

I didn't sleep well for about the next ten days. My mind would be consumed with every possible angle and outcome, and what the future may bring. Before I went to sleep, I would think about the possibilities of the chat that we needed to have with our parents. If I woke in the middle of the night, and when I woke in the morning, I would be consumed by my thoughts. My mind conjectured everything conceivable.

During the daytime, I would yawn constantly and move about my day in a daze. The worst part was that I was snappy with Angus and our children. The tiredness made me become someone I was not, or at least someone that I had not been since I was a teenager in charge of my siblings. I had to do something, and I had to do it soon.

'Knowing is not enough ...' But was it—we had to decide if we wanted to know more.

That was the biggest question of all. I started to contact my siblings. 'What are we going to do?' I asked each of them.

We all had time to consider our options over the past few days. The choice was easy. Unanimously, we decided to see if we could find our sibling.

But before we did that, we would have to talk to our parents ...

I asked them all if they wanted to chat with our parents. Not all of us could or wanted to face our parents. It was decided that Angus, Cynthia, Billie and I would be the ones to talk to Mum and Dad. The following weekend would be The Day that could change our world.

Would they lie and deny, as my grandfather predicted? What could they say? I wondered whether they'd be shocked, pleased or relieved that we were finally going to know. How would they react? Maybe, at long last, they'd be glad they could speak to us about it openly. Or was that too much wishful thinking?

I tried not to think about their reactions, good or bad. But it was hard not to. What if they refused all communication and told us to get out? What if, what if, so many possibilities.

Ultimately, we had to wait and see.

I was excited yet scared and apprehensive; a mixture of all of those emotions and more. There was no doubt that I was in the bargaining stage of grief. Bargaining or begging them to tell us the truth, in their own words. Could they be honest with us? We deserved that, surely.

In a few short days, we could know some of the answers to our questions. We didn't know the truth all these years. Could I wait a few more days?

Chapter 4
SECRET REVEALED

*To know that one has a secret is to know half
the secret itself.* —Henry Ward Beecher

THE DAY

The night before, I couldn't sleep. I tried adjusting myself and closing my eyes before listening to relaxation music and meditation. Finally, counting and tapping distracted my mind enough to allow me to melt into the slumber and peacefulness of sleep.

In the morning, I woke as soon as the sun peeked through the blinds in my bedroom. I nervously opened my eyes with the realisation that today was The Day.

The truth was in my parents' hands. Will the truth set them free with a few words? Or would they deny or refuse to answer, leaving us with more pain?

I thought about the fact that a secret shared can put your mind at rest, the burden would be gone, and they would be able to let it go at last. I wondered if my parents would feel that way.

I contacted the Benevolent Society the day before to discuss this situation. They provide support services for those affected by past adoptions. Angelina was the lady I had contact with. She gave good advice by email. She said, 'Try to listen to their reactions without "pushing back" too hard in this first conversation. Let them have their say and then go away to think about "what next."'

Our parents were old now. My mother was sixty-seven and my father was eighty. Life had not fared well for either of them. My mother walked slowly, often with the aid of a wheelie-walker. Our father was unwell, though we did not know why. Regardless, he always determined if we needed to know or not. Not just when it came to their health, but with all aspects of their lives.

It was only in 2025 that I learnt from a nurse at one of my mother's hospital admissions that mum had a severe arm fracture around the time all this was happening in 2014. When I asked her about it, she said she fell. It was another secret that had only just come to light. I felt sorry for her when I heard about this, regardless of how it happened.

Their home at the time of our visit was so far away from hospitals or facilities needed by an elderly couple. Our father was driving, although he should not have been. We found out sometime later that he had not renewed his driver's licence for around ten years, though I don't know why. Our mother had not driven by choice for some years.

My father was a very stubborn and harsh man when he wanted to be. When he said something, most of the time, that was that. Even when I was a teenager, my mother would ask me to ask him to change the TV channel. I never questioned why; I would just ask him. It seemed so weird in retrospect.

When we were growing up, our parents often fought quite forcefully and vocally. Towards the end of a fight, my mother would often ask my father for the keys to the car. He usually had hidden them and wouldn't tell her where they were. There were times when I sensed their fights could escalate to physical violence. I would hide under the covers in my bed until the yelling stopped.

Maybe she did want the keys to leave. Maybe it was alcohol related. Whatever the reason, and in the light of the new day, the leaving impulse or the fear of the unknown may have gone. I don't know, but I do wonder.

When remembering this side of my parents, and especially my father, I was concerned about how they would react when we talked to them. Even after we left, what would they think, or do? Would they argue as I'd witnessed in the past, or would the house fall silent? That I didn't know either.

When thinking about all the scenarios, we agreed that we would not go in accusing or demanding. We would go in with empathy, seeking the truth. If they denied us the information, which was a strong possibility, we might have to accept that for the time being. In my heart, I could feel a tightness, a dull ache that they wouldn't tell us the truth.

We knew that if that was the case, and they either would not talk to us or they would not confide in us, we could find the information we needed elsewhere. If we did look elsewhere, and we discovered that they had not told the truth, we could talk to our parents and say, 'Remember when you did not tell us the truth?'

Before going to our parents' house for our chat, Cynthia and Billie met Angus and me at our home. We talked about what we thought the day would bring. We tried to put ourselves in their shoes. Our father used to tell us, 'Put yourself in the other person's shoes.' I don't think he lived by that rule himself.

Regardless, we tried to imagine an eighty-year-old man and his sixty-seven-year-old wife being asked if they had another child. A child whom they had chosen to keep a secret.

There was no way of knowing what mood our father would be in until we arrived. We could get the dad who would be a happy, jovial dad who liked to joke around with other people. The worst-case scenario would be the defensive dad, who would become angry and dark-eyed. His facial expression would tell us immediately which dad we would face.

Cynthia and I agreed that our grandfather had not lied about this. We decided we wouldn't reveal to our parents who told us about this. That was not our place. We weren't there to start an argument or feud between our parents and our aunt. We just wanted to know the truth for our possible sibling and us.

My dad had another saying, 'Don't play with fire.' It felt like we might have been.

But as Billie drove us to our parents' home, Angus held my shaking hand. I was feeling numb and sick to the pit of my stomach. My shoulders were hunched as I tried to concentrate on my breath. None of us spoke. Cynthia and I were lost in our own thoughts and fears.

Trying to focus on anything other than what was going on inside my head, I looked out the car window, trying to calm the overwhelming feeling of panic and dread. I took extra notice of the hectic traffic hindered by the roadworks, the cheering parents at the sporting event at the local high school and even the new sign on the building of one of my old workplaces as we drove by.

We hadn't called our parents to let them know we were coming. That in itself was a gamble. What if they weren't home? If they were out, shopping or something, we would have to get the courage up to do it another day. I don't think we even contemplated that possibility.

Thankfully for us, they were home when we knocked on their door. I am sure that they wondered why we were there. We did not come for unannounced visits, especially the four of us. Mum seemed unperturbed; I think she was glad to see us all. Dad, on the other hand, stared at me and then at Cynthia like he was trying to decipher why we were there. We didn't give anything away, and so he offered us a cup of tea or coffee.

It gave me a chance to look at him unnoticed. He looked terrible. He was gaunt, thin and pale. While he made the cuppas in the kitchen, I asked Mum if he was okay.

She said, 'He's been trying to lose weight.'

At that time, the only person who thought that he was overweight was himself. One thing I did know about him was that he and his twin brother had been diagnosed with diabetes a few years before. Since then, he became even more obsessed with his diet and weight. At that stage of his life, he did not need to lose weight.

'I think he thinks he is helping his diabetes,' she continued.

After the cuppas were made, we all sat around the dining table. It was a wonder that I did not fall off my seat as I was sitting so close to the edge. My arms were rigid, and my hands gripped the edge of the seat beside my legs until my knuckles were white. I had to steady my breath before anyone noticed. The discussion I dreaded moved closer and closer.

The jovial father emerged by starting the conversation with jokes. He would always joke when he was unsure what to say or to lighten the mood. I was not listening to his words, but I laughed on cue.

Cynthia managed to steer the conversation away from the jokes. 'We actually came here for a serious conversation. We've found out some information, and we need you to be honest,' she paused. 'We've been told that you had another child before all of us,' she said.

Silence. Like a lightning bolt. The quietness was deafening. I could hear the noise of a car engine revving in the distance.

Then, with a crack, my father slammed his clenched fist down hard onto the wooden surface of the table, the vibrating noise interrupting the stillness. His facial expression had changed from jovial to one of anger and full of rage.

'What a load of crap, who told you that?' he said as he got up and walked away from the table.

My heart was pumping so fast, and I could feel my hands becoming hot and sweaty. My mind went blank. I could not find any words. Cynthia kicked my leg under the table, and then she looked at me. Somehow, I managed to find the words that I needed.

'We are only asking you out of concern,' I said.

'And please, we want you to be honest,' Cynthia said quickly. She, too, looked flustered.

'It's about information that you two may have,' I said with nervousness in my voice. 'That you had another child before I was born.'

My dad returned to the table, and he repeated, 'Where did you hear that from?'

'That's not the question right now, but why would someone say something as huge as that?' I asked.

Cynthia said, 'If it isn't true, that's not a nice thing to say.'

Mum sat still; she remained completely silent. The four of us looked at each other, noticing the stunned look on our faces. I didn't know whether to sit there and cry or walk away. No one knew what to say or do. We sat still firmly in our seats.

After what seemed like forever, Dad proceeded to tell another joke. I remember the joke being about a woman who had memory loss and lost her baby. I think she found the baby in the roof. What ...?

I looked around the room, as if the answer would appear somewhere. My dad's words were like a jolt to my stomach, a bit like an electric shock running through me. My mouth became dry as I clenched my fists under the table. How dare he dodge our question. All he wanted to know was who told us. It was not good enough to leave things that way.

After my father paused at the end of his joke, I didn't allow him to say another word. I took the plunge, looking directly at our mother who remained silent, and I said, 'Mum, can you tell me if it's true or not?'

She looked down as if she was feeling shame and murmured, 'Yes, it is.'

After those three words, Cynthia and I looked at each other. Our mouths dropped open.

Our mother looked up and said, 'It was a son, and we never wanted you to know.'

Cynthia said, 'Thank you for being honest.'

Those words, 'we never wanted you to know,' were harder to hear than the truth. My goodness, how could they knowingly do that? They'd held the truth from us, and they had no intention of letting us know, ever!

Our father then interrupted my thoughts and said, 'It couldn't have come on a worse day.'

'Why, what is today?' I said, thinking it was a significant day unknown to us.

Mum said, 'I had a bit of a turn today.' She told us that she had some health issues. I do not recall the issues, but I did realise that it was nothing major to worry about at that moment. I was way too consumed with the revelation, and nothing could distract me from that.

The conversation went back to the sibling that we now knew we had.

'Mum, you could have told us when Nancy turned 18, but since you didn't, can you tell us when he was born?' Cynthia said.

Dad said to Mum, 'No, it's in the past, let it lie.' Then he turned to us and said, 'You don't need to dig it up.'

I said, 'This affects us too. It was our sibling. Maybe Mum wants to talk about it.'

Dad asked her if she wanted to talk about it, and she said, 'No.'

Cynthia and I told them that it was important for us to know; this is part of our heritage, and there may be other implications. What if our child came across that person's child and had a relationship? What if they had health issues we needed to know about? We were trying to draw attention to the bigger picture.

'Hogwash!' Dad said.

Our mother opened up a little and said, 'He would have gone to a good Catholic home because he went to the nuns near the hospital in Melbourne.'

That little piece of knowledge about her son probably helped her feel a bit better for all those years.

'So, he was born in Melbourne?' I asked.

'Yes.'

My eyes welled up. I looked at Cynthia, who was also stunned and teary-eyed. I took a deep breath. I could not look at my parents; instead, I glared at the ceiling.

'What you must have gone through. We can understand a little bit more now,' I said as I tried to pull myself together.

Cynthia and I tried to let them know that we were not judging them. We tried to show empathy for what they must have gone through. We also wanted them to know that we had to digest the information and deal with it in our own way.

Our father's face remained an unmistakable, blazing crimson filled with anger. He glared at us and returned to the question of who had told us. In the past, he would glare at us like that, and we would have crumbled. But not this time. We held fast in our decision not to reveal and throw our Aunty into the deep end. He had lost his sense of control, and that made him angrier.

My mind returned to numbness. I could hear what I thought was polite conversation, like it was being said in the distance, and I could not focus on the words. I did not utter another word.

We had been unsure if they would answer our question. But they had. I was overwhelmed. I just wanted to leave. One of us thanked them for the cuppas as we walked outside to the car.

Just as I will always remember the words of the truth spoken that day, I will always remember the look on my mum's face as we pulled out of their driveway. It was one of pure anguish. Looking back, I think we were all shocked by the level of truth they told.

At that time, our father called out to us, 'He could be in jail or on drugs.'

Sometime later, I realised and understood that my father was possibly scared of what we might discover about our sibling. He was not immune to fear.

Our parents had family friends who had adopted a child. Not only did they have to see that child being raised in another family and feel the pangs of despair, but they also witnessed the outcome when that child tried to find his birth parents as an adult. Suffice to say, it did not end well.

We drove away with the confirmation that our parents had lied to us all our lives. There was no denying that anymore, no hiding or covering it up any longer.

A moment later, Angus grabbed my hand once again and said to me, 'How do you feel about that?'

'I don't want to say anything until we are completely away from here,' I said, my voice quivering.

It was a few minutes until I was able to respond to Angus.

'F**k!' I said, and Cynthia and I cried.

Over the next couple of days, I tried to digest the news as best I could. I was trying to detach myself from the feelings. I wanted to hide, but I couldn't hide from the overwhelming sadness and the sluggishness that came with it. I thought I'd already started the grieving process, and I had. But knowing that it was true made it harder and more real. I felt heartache for my siblings and my older brother. I even managed to feel some sadness for my mother and father.

This was when I started to think, 'how dare you?'

I played the blame game, and no one was exempt. Yes, it seems harsh writing it here, but that is what contributed to this dark part of our history. From those close to me—my parents and grandparents, and their small-town community. To those I did not even know—the workers who contributed to taking babies from their mothers directly after birth, the homes or institutions that housed unmarried mothers, society in general and the government for their treatment of them.

Due to the child being born illegitimate, society at the time was unsympathetic to unmarried, single mothers, regardless of their situation. It was not a new problem in the late 1960s, but when my brother was born, it affected our family. Never did I dream that we would discover that our family was part of that. So unnecessary, so unfair.

I came across a Four Corners report about closed adoptions, 'Given or Taken.' At the height of the practice, nearly 10,000 babies were given up for adoption in one year. Advocacy groups estimated that up to 250,000 children were given up for adoption, and many more lives were deeply affected. These mothers, who were not married, despite some being engaged, were given a fate, a torment, an existence stripped of all joy, that no one should endure. Aside from the coercive practices, they were often isolated, broken, punished, drugged, shackled to their beds, and traumatised in a way that was cruel and unjust.[4]

My mother was one of these women. The happiest moments of her life, the normalcy of the birth of her first child, were taken from her. Such were the societal demands, the shame and stigma that my mother's life would have been changed from that point forward. She would have experienced deep sorrow, unable to escape from the pain and trauma of not knowing or seeing her son.

I will remain sad for her.

Chapter 5
TO FIND COMPASSION OR NOT?

Girls who became pregnant outside marriage in the fifties and sixties immediately lost caste. Whatever their previous status they were now bad girls who had to be kept apart from their more respectable sisters. — Shurlee Swain[5]

Not only did they strip the baby away from my mother, but they also metaphorically took my mother away from her future babies—us. When I was born, as the first baby they could take home, they had nothing left. No maternal instinct, just the effects of shame and torment. The repercussions of those events have been felt for decades.

For my mother in her day, pregnancy outside marriage effectively ensured a life sentence. Simply because of a lack of a marriage certificate, a simple piece of paper, the mother was deemed unfit to raise her child. The details were covered up as if it had not happened. But it did. My mother was termed a bad girl, a lost caste—titles I am sure she did not appreciate. And yet my parents were the ones who had to struggle with giving up a child. They had to live every day without seeing their child's smile. They did not know where he lived or if he was happy, safe and content with life.

I am not sure in what order the events followed for my parents. Was it the engagement or the pregnancy announcement? Regardless, both of these should have been times of celebration. But they were not. I found out a great deal of this later on, after I found my brother.

My mother fell pregnant, and they were not married.

In those days, it was pretty hard to cover up a pregnancy and get married. It would have the same outcome as if they had married after the child's birth. A mother could plead with the authorities about her impending wedding, but it made no difference. The child would still be given up for adoption.

My father, being a divorcee, made matters worse. In the 1960s, marrying a man who had been married before was considered unacceptable. That was the first issue that brought disrespect to my mother's family. The second, of course, was the child born out of wedlock.

When my parents told my grandparents that my mother was carrying a child, my mother's family reacted the way society dictated. They were banished from the family home for the term of the pregnancy. I believe this was partly due to what the neighbours would think, but also my mother had two younger sisters who looked up to her. They were the 'respectable sisters', and my mother was not.

Together, these issues would have been catastrophic for my parents.

After the revelation of my mother's pregnancy at the farm that day, my grandparents took my mother's four siblings to church as normal to maintain the appearance of the ideal strong family unit, characterised by good morals. Except that day was not normal. Normally, when my parents joined the family for a church service, my mum's siblings chose to sit with them. During the service that day, her siblings kept looking back for them to arrive, but they did not show up.

Instead, they were back at home, removing all of my mother's belongings from her bedroom, including any photos. I am guessing her parents told her to get her things and go. After the church service, when the family returned home, her siblings went into my mother's room, only to notice that all her things had gone and so had she.

One day, I asked my mother if my grandparents were supportive of her pregnancy. She merely replied, 'Yes, but they did not want me to go to the farm until after the birth, so the others wouldn't see me pregnant.'

Without the support of her family, each milestone would have been met with silence and with the knowledge that she would be giving up the baby after birth.

The birth would have been a sterile, traumatic and isolating event. I do not know much about my mother's birthing experience. She does not talk about it. But some mothers were even physically restrained or shackled to their beds during and after delivery. Aside from possible abusive practices and the lack of medical care, there was the mental anguish and the trauma that they suffered. The baby was then taken away for a closed adoption process. My mother could not find out any details from then on.

My brother was born a couple of years and ten days before me. The consent to adopt was signed five days after his birth.

As far as her impending wedding to my father, she tried to win the approval and blessing of her parents. She wrote a letter to Pope Paul VI asking for his permission to marry a divorcee. Among other ideals, the Pope strongly advocated social justice. Yet, a response was not received.

I am sure she was still grieving, but six weeks after the birth of the baby and taken away from my mother, my parents got married. We found out later that he was also placed in the care of his adoptive parents on the same day as my parents' wedding. They would not have been aware of this at the time. Regardless, it would have been bittersweet, with the joy of completing their nuptials, but it was also a time for sorrow and devastating change.

My grandparents arrived before my parents' wedding to stop the wedding. There was a discussion with my father and grandfather. My grandfather eventually agreed to the marriage. However, my mum's parents and most of her siblings did not witness the ceremony. One of my uncles snuck into the service to witness the wedding. My grandparents, aunts and uncles went to the reception afterwards. They sourced clothes to wear, and on the day, the reception centre had to find more chairs so they could sit down with everyone else.

Sometime after my parents' wedding, a new era began, a time of acceptance for the relationship between my parents and grandparents. The past was in the past, and they were able to move forward, somewhat.

As I wrote this, I felt empathy for my mother. She endured a lifetime of pain and uncertainty as a result of a few moments of lust. I was beginning to understand why she is the way she is, resulting, in part, from such a tragedy. The shame and guilt she would have suffered would be insurmountable and incomprehensible to me and anyone else who has not experienced giving up their child.

The trauma of not knowing her first child is inconceivable. She knew that her child was out there; she just could not see him, ever. That has got to be one of the most awful things to happen to a young person learning how to become a woman. Additionally, she had to cope with being rejected by her family.

I was given a book, *A Refuge at Kildare: The History of the Geelong Female Refuge and Bethany Babies Home* by Shurlee Swain. This book acknowledged these young ladies and their struggles, 'Perhaps if society had had more adequate support systems some of these painful decisions need not have been made but in the fifties and sixties no such systems existed.'[6]

And yet, my grandparents watched and allowed this to happen to my mother, their own child. They did what they thought was right in the moment, simply by following society's demands. But, at what cost to themselves, their daughter and the person that was to be their first grandchild? Even if society dictated, how could a daughter ever forget such intense feelings of rejection, abandonment and shame?

We kept regular telephone contact with our mother once we knew about our sibling. A few weeks later, after we'd originally talked with my parents, we wanted to check in with her. Cynthia and I decided to pick her up from her Friday morning craft group and take her for a coffee in a local café. We chose a location away from her home and our father, so we could talk freely with her.

Inside the café, we chose a table that was away from others so we could talk in privacy. We all ordered a coffee. Our mother usually only had one black coffee with two sugars a day. But on that day, she had a second. I ordered a latte, and Cynthia ordered a chai latte. The conversation started slowly with talk about Cynthia's recent family holiday and my son's school trip to the snow. We were talking about anything other than what we had come here for.

What we also wanted to achieve that day was more understanding, to ask more questions, and hopefully to receive truthful responses and answers. Our mother may give us that, away from our father.

Eventually, we addressed the elephant in the room, and we began the conversation we needed to have.

'How are you going with the fact that we know about the adoption?' I asked Mum.

'Yeah ...' she replied.

'It must have been a shock that we knew,' Cynthia said.

'Yes,' she said.

We asked her if she wondered why we had turned up at her home the day that we asked the question. She told us that she had thought nothing of it.

'Has Dad spoken much about it?' Cynthia asked Mum.

'On the day, yes. Since then, no,' Mum said.

'Dad always used to tell us to put ourselves in the other person's shoes. He's not putting himself in our shoes. We are trying to put ourselves in your shoes as much as we can by being understanding and empathetic. We realise that it must have been really hard; times were different then,' I said.

'We don't hold any judgment towards you. We only want to be supportive, but Dad is not being supportive towards us,' Cynthia said.

We told Mum about the Four Corners program, where we found out about closed adoptions. It had given us some greater insight into Mum and what she must have gone through.

We told her about a story of a mother from the program, who had knitted her son a jumper for every year of his life until he would have turned twenty-one. If he came looking for her, he would know by that she had loved and cared about him.

Previously, such adoptions were closed, which meant that the child's original birth certificate was sealed forever. They thought this would give a clean break between mother and baby. Instead, the mothers endured a lifetime of heartache, sorrow, pain and shame.

Cynthia and I were mothers ourselves. Cynthia has two children; I have three children and two stepchildren. I could not imagine having to give my child up directly after birth without seeing their face or touching and holding them. Not being able to see them grow with each milestone and love them unconditionally is inconceivable to me.

My third child was taken from me after birth and put into a humidicrib because he had pneumonia. I could still see and touch my child. Initially, I had to go home without him, but he was well enough for me to take him home after five days. If I couldn't take him home, my heart would have crumbled. I didn't know it at the time—but my experience was hardly comparable to what my mother experienced.

She barely got to hold her son after his birth. She did not feed him, change his nappy or watch him sleep in wonderment at what she had created. He was swiftly taken from her, along with the chance to see him again. Back then, it was for the term of their lives.

Hopefully and at last, we could help our mum meet him, know him and acknowledge him as her son. That was something that no one had been able to give to her until now.

Towards the end of our coffee conversation that day, our mother told us that David, our youngest brother, had told her that we had started searching for our older brother. I guess she also wanted to know what had happened to her son. In her way, I am sure she was excited.

We confirmed that we had contacted the department in Melbourne. At the time, I was not sure why she looked a bit nervous or unsure about what we would discover. As we drove her home, we reassured her that we would keep her updated with any information we found out.

I have a few people that I turn to when I need to talk—Angus, my sisters, girlfriends and workmates. I often want to get a different point of view. Sometimes it's general day-to-day things, other times it is something positive, or negative, and sometimes fear-based that I would want to talk about or decide on. I couldn't imagine being unable to talk to them about things.

I struggled with someone leaving information in a closed vault hoping it would never be revealed. I hoped that, being with Cynthia and me in a public place, our mother would want to talk. Even to get it off her chest. She didn't. Any information she shared with us that day was limited or filled with holes, creating more questions. We did not push her further. It may have been too painful to go back there. Perhaps she had not overcome the feeling of shame.

'Shame is an emotion that involves negative self-evaluation ... You may believe that you haven't lived up to certain standards and feel unworthy or inadequate as a result. Shame often operates outside of conscious awareness, making it challenging to identify and overcome—but healing and growth are always possible.'[7]

I think my mother remained paralysed by her shame. Her self-esteem became so low that I do not think she ever recovered from it. It's quite possible she was experiencing all of that shame flooding back to her now that we knew.

I wondered if she was like that because she had pushed the memories so far down into her vault, hiding the traumatic recollections and hoping that they would stay there. Or was it that she considered, relived and thought about it every single day? Even if she had thought about it, she had never talked about it before now. None of her siblings or friends knew. The subject was completely taboo. She had a shared experience with my father, but how often did they talk about it? Possibly, our father wanted it to stay in the past.

The pain, the anguish, the possible repressed memories and the shame—how do we cope with that? In a lot of cases, we may live in the present, keeping ourselves busy, using avoidance tactics like addiction to suppress the loss. Our mother was often avoidant. She was not there; her soul suppressed, and she was unable to give to her other children what we needed.

She was not callous. She cared and she loved us in her way. She unknowingly protected herself by doing the best she could with what she had left. Could I find compassion? To some extent, for what she had gone through. But not for what we got, the part of her that was left. We got the blankness, the bits left. She could not enjoy and be grateful for what she had.

Although it may feel harsh, all I ever wanted was a mum.

My dad, well, he was different. With thirteen years of life experience, you would think that he was wise and old enough to fight. Maybe he didn't have any fight left. I will never know if everything played out the way he wanted. He'd had a failed marriage, a life lived and lost before my mother entered his life. Does this excuse his behaviour?

As a teen, I could talk to him when he was being a normal dad. He used to say, 'Blast you!' in a good way. We knew it as his way of us getting under his skin and his way of saying, 'I love you.' That was how he could best express his feelings. Through it all, my mother continued and continues to defend his behaviour. She is enduringly loyal to him, whether he deserves it or not.

He could be a nice person when he wanted to. I do not believe that he was always the hard man that we saw often. He had the gift of the gab; he could be charming, even to those he should not have charmed. At some point, possibly as a result of all the demons and bad times in his life, he must have put up his defences to become someone else entirely. He became an abuser, a harsh man within his own home. There were many things that he should not have done. I've said it already, but these things, I'm not yet ready to write about.

But could I have compassion for him? I did have empathy for what he had been through when my brother was taken from them. I could not have compassion for the way he was as a father, nor could I have compassion for the way he treated us when we discovered the truth. Not yet.

Can I find compassion for him? I am working on all of that. As I write these words, I am realising a bit more empathy and understanding. Time will tell.

My parents did do the best they could. It was what they were left with. Was that the best for the five of us? Probably not.

I will say that my mother was not 'a bad girl.' That was merely society's opinion. Cruel, unsympathetic and uncalled for. My father, although he remained the other person in this scenario, was lucky that he did not bear the brunt of such opinions as much as my mother did.

Chapter 6

STARTING THE SEARCH

I do not want to have the humongous regrets … the little
ones I could learn from, the big ones will be heartbreaking.

JUNE 2014

To say that I was nervous, apprehensive and scared about the next step was an understatement. We were about to look for our brother, and we knew that it came with risk. I was not dealing with the situation very well, as I continued to mourn for what was meant to be. Cynthia and David also struggled, but were there every step of the way. Jennifer and Nancy were also, but not as involved in the everyday details. I valued their support, and the support we gave each other. While I can only write about how I personally felt, each of my siblings carried their own level of distress, grief and challenges. We all felt the weight deeply, though we each coped and dealt with it in our own ways. Despite how we were feeling, we had to find out more information.

In a bid to try to help each of us with our pain, I had contacted Angelina from the Benevolent Society by phone and email. She said they could give us post-adoption support from within their Queensland office. All of us, my siblings and our parents, could seek guidance from them if we wanted. Angelina also advised me on what the department needed and how to start it all. She could even contact them on our behalf first.

What became apparent quickly was that, as full siblings, we would be entitled to get non-identifying information, such as his birth name and the first name given to him by his adoptive parents. If it were our parents or our brother seeking this information, they would be entitled to access more details. Angelina forwarded me the application that we would have to send to the department, and she emailed me a brochure about their service.

The Family Information, Networks, and Discovery Department (FIND) was based in Melbourne and is now known as Adoption Information Services. It falls under the Department of Justice and Community Safety. Through them, we could find out more about the steps we needed to take and how they could assist us in finding our brother. My mind raced. What if he did not know that he was adopted? Regardless, he probably was not aware that he had five siblings. If he didn't know, he might be about to have his world rocked. We could be there for him if that were the case. But were we being selfish by searching for him?

What if he had looked for us before, without success? We had moved around a lot, which would have made finding us more difficult. Did our parents move around so much that we could not be found?

Then again, if we didn't search, we might never know. After all, if we found him, he could choose to say no and not have contact with us. That outcome could prove even more heartbreaking for us all.

Despite the risks to our brother and us, we decided, as a collective of the five of us, that we would move forward with our search. I hoped and prayed that we would have a happy ending.

As the eldest of the five siblings, I contacted the department, FIND, on 13 June 2014.

I received a call from the department one week later. They had assigned a case worker, Brenda, to our case. She advised that the process had begun and how it would work. It could take several weeks before we knew anything at all. I was happy that Brenda had been assigned to our case. She was empathetic and understanding. She asked how we were all doing with the news.

I knew that it was going to take time, but at that time, patience was not a virtue I possessed. So, I rang Brenda again in early July. She told me that no new information had come to hand and said that it might be another one or two weeks.

Waiting and waiting ...

The more I thought about things, the more questions I had. I was sure that my four siblings also had their questions. I contacted them, and we decided that it would be a good idea to have a collective phone meeting with Brenda. That way we could ask any of those questions and get the information that we needed firsthand, rather than me relaying everything from Brenda.

Getting a date, time, and place took a while to organise. But, like everything else in this process to that point, we worked it out.

JULY 2014

Our chat with Brenda was organised at David and his wife Rose's home in Brisbane. Cynthia, Billie, Angus and I joined them there.

After introducing Brenda to the others, we asked her if we could tape the conversation. She replied yes. Then we started our conversation. Firstly, Brenda explained that, as our brother's siblings, we were entitled to the bare minimum of information. She had that information. But she hoped to get any other information from the records at the adoption agency. Unfortunately, she was unable to find anything else.

Our questions came quickly after that. One of the main questions we had was whether the records stated the name of the natural father. In other words, did it show our father's name on the birth certificate? We were not concerned with the outcome of this; we knew that our father was the natural father. We just wanted to know what the birth certificate stated.

'Are you able to release the names of both parents that were on the birth certificate?' Rose asked.

Brenda confirmed that only our mother's name was listed on the birth certificate.

'So does that mean that the father was shown as unknown, or that there was nothing recorded about him?' Cynthia asked.

Brenda clarified that if a child was born out of wedlock, only the natural mother's name would go on the birth certificate. This applied to all births up until the 1980s. Even if our mother stood at the counter and said they were partners and that they were going to get married one day and have more children, Births, Deaths, and Marriages would not have shown him on the certificate as the father.

Brenda moved on to telling us about the information from the Court Summary: Natural Relative. The information we were entitled to included some of his adoption details—he was six weeks old when placed in the care of his adoptive parents. We were eager to know the name our brother had been given by his adoptive parents—they named him Saul, and his date of birth was 11 February.

The right to name the child was not always given to the natural mother, but our mother had been given that right. She named him Robert James. My paternal and maternal grandfathers were both called

Robert, and James was my maternal grandfather's middle name. But his adoptive parents had called him Saul.

David asked, 'The six weeks from when he was born until being adopted out, do you know any information about that?'

Brenda confirmed Saul had been born in Geelong, though the court records were not clear whether he remained in the Geelong hospital for those entire six weeks until he was adopted, or if they moved him to Melbourne. The adoption agency may have temporarily placed him in one of the nurseries or with a foster carer until he went home with his new parents. But our mother was not with him or caring for him.

David added, 'I thought he was born in Melbourne, that's what my mother told me.'

Brenda said that the records showed he was born in Geelong.

David asked, 'Is the adoption agency Catholic? Our mother believed that a Catholic family had adopted him.'

Brenda let us know that it was not.

'Oh!' David said.

'So were the adoptive parents Catholic?' I asked.

Brenda said they assumed his adoptive parents were Anglican because they were married in an Anglican Church.

'Can you tell us if he has searched for us?' Cynthia asked.

Brenda advised us that he had not registered with the service to make any enquiries about his adoption. The Department held a central registry for such enquiries since the 1980s. Anyone who asked about an adoption went on this register, and his name was not on it.

Brenda explained that there were three other smaller church-based services in Victoria, similar to FIND, that could also assist with past adoptions. The services were obliged to let the department know if anyone contacted them about an adoption so that they could add their details to the register. Saul hadn't attended any of those services either.

'So, there's no other agency; just those three and you guys?' David asked.

Brenda confirmed this because they were Victorian-based records.

'Can you tell us if he's alive?' Cynthia asked as she fidgeted in her seat.

She said that they didn't know. But, if we were happy for her to search for him, then she would, explaining that FIND liaised with Births, Deaths and Marriages in Victoria. They would also tell her if there was any record of marriage. If Saul's family had moved interstate, she asked for our patience because it would take longer.

'So, you don't know what his surname is?' Cynthia asked.

Brenda said she knew his name, but as it was identifying information, she would be unable to give it to us.

'So, what do we do from here? What's the next step?' Cynthia asked.

Brenda asked if we wanted to have contact with Saul, should that be an option.

'Yes!' Cynthia and David said firmly, nodding.

Brenda advised us that if we located Saul, she would send him a letter. She said that she would be happy to do that with or without our parents being involved. As natural relatives, we were legally able to have this contact. Brenda strongly recommended that we sit down with our folks, if possible, and try to chat further with them.

'We plan on doing that,' Cynthia said.

Brenda added that if Mum wanted to, she was welcome to call her and chat about this at any time. It might even be a positive thing for her to do.

'So, if, for instance, Mum didn't want to talk to you in person, but she felt comfortable emailing you, could she do that?' Cynthia asked.

Brenda said she could communicate with her any way she liked.

'What other common types of questions do people in our situation ask right about now?' Rose asked.

Brenda informed us that we'd asked the main ones. The one question that she could not answer then was whether the adoptee knew about his adoption. It was often a big worry or question mark when starting these searches. In our situation, as Saul had not registered with the department, she couldn't say with one hundred per cent certainty whether or not he knew that he was adopted.

'How does that usually turn out?' Cynthia asked.

Brenda replied that around a dozen adoptees per year didn't know they were adopted. She said that despite their shock at finding out, many of them suspected they were adopted because they didn't look like anyone in the family. She couldn't tell us how Saul might react to our request for contact. He might or might not want to engage with us.

Cynthia asked Brenda if they offered counselling as part of the service. Brenda said yes, they did, and to let her know if any of us wanted to take advantage of it.

If Brenda found our brother, she advised that she would call me, as the main contact, to let me know. Then she would send him a letter explaining that there had been a personal enquiry relating to his family and asking if he would like to get in touch.

We all looked at each other and listened intently. This was now getting very real.

People usually call back pretty quickly, Brenda told us. She would explain to him that the enquiry was from his natural-born siblings. She would keep us posted the whole way, suggesting that if Saul agreed to having contact, one of us could act as the spokesperson. It might be incredibly overwhelming for him to have contact with several siblings all at once. We needed to ensure that, however we made contact, he felt comfortable with it.

'You said that his adoptive dad was a baker's apprentice, is that right?' Rose asked.

From the records she had, Brenda thought that it meant that he may have been doing deliveries for one of the bakeries in Melbourne.

'Was it normal back then for the adoption papers to take eight to nine months?' I asked.

Brenda elaborated on what she said earlier—that Saul had been taken to his adoptive parents' home at six weeks—and the formal adoption took place eight months later. She advised it was completely normal and highly likely our mum wasn't told that his name became Saul. Neither would she have known when or where he was taken.

'So, you don't know any address details for him at the moment, do you?' I asked nervously. 'That's probably a silly question!' I was clutching at straws.

Brenda confirmed that she did not know. She said that she could start the process next week to get further information, once we gave her the okay to proceed.

'With the Do Not Contact part of things, if Dad wasn't listed on the birth certificate, he couldn't have done a DNC, is that right?' I asked. I wanted to understand this part of the process, as I believed that our father would have done so if he could.

On Saul's records, Brenda verified that no DNC was listed. Because of this, we were right that our father had no legal right to decline contact. Furthermore, we could have contact with him: he is our brother.

'Brenda, when we go and talk to Mum and Dad next, do you have any advice that we could use to help with our chat with them?' Cynthia asked.

Brenda suggested that first, we have to think about why we want to pursue this. She asked if we thought we had the space in our lives to welcome a brother, or, at best, would we exchange cards at Christmas. She suggested that if we could answer those questions, our wishes would be a bit clearer. Then we could talk to our parents. She advised us to try to forgive our parents for not sharing the news with us. She said that we needed to be patient with them, especially since they'd carried this secret for a long time. The fact that we were going to sit down and talk with them would in itself be enormous for them.

She added that some or all of us were probably still adjusting to the news. Especially me, because I was no longer the eldest. She was right. Hearing those words was weird. What would it all mean? I was still coming to terms with it all.

Why *did* we want to find our brother? Above all, he was part of our family—our brother, the older brother that I had always wanted. I might no longer be the eldest, and yes, our relationship would be different to what it would have been had we been raised together, but I felt that we had a right to get to know each other as siblings. Things like medical history, where we came from and who we are now are important. Even knowing how his parents raised him, some of his milestones, the type of person he was as a child and now. I wanted the chance to love my brother for who he is. There was no doubt in my mind.

I knew that was all about me and how I felt. I hope that he knew about his adoption and that he truly felt the same way. That we would be able to know him and he would know us.

'For me, one of the hardest things is thinking that our parents could have been married because Mum was twenty-one. Do you know what the laws were back then? Did you only need parental consent to get married if you were under twenty-one?' I asked.

She said she wasn't sure. She had seen records of girls aged seventeen and eighteen who were married. Brenda asked us when our folks got married.

'March 13,' I replied. 'Saul was born on February 11, then I was born on February 1 two years later. The closeness of these dates is something I'm going to find hard to cope with, and I think he would too!' I spoke.

Brenda acknowledged that this changed things, especially what we knew about our folks and our identity within the family.

'We don't know whether Saul's birth was early or late,' I said. 'He could have been premature, since the four of us girls were all pre-term births. I was three weeks early; Nancy was about three months premature.'

Brenda asked if we thought the child was born in January.

'Well, we were told it was January or December,' I said.

'A lot of the information you've told us conflicts with what Mum told us,' Cynthia added.

Brenda said that time did funny things to people's minds and explained that she had worked with a natural mother who'd had twins. She forgot she had had twins; she just remembered one. And another mother whose baby was born in 1975, and she thought it was 1978. She said that the experience and the trauma of someone being separated from their baby that they'd carried for nine months had a significant impact on these women.

Our mum probably wouldn't have meant to mislead us in any way; she probably genuinely believed what she told us, she just got mixed up. Brenda encouraged us to be patient with our mother—it was strongly likely, in her eyes, that what she said was right.

'Okay,' we replied.

Brenda asked if we had any other questions.

'When we give you the go-ahead for the search, how long will it take?' Cynthia asked.

She said that if they could locate the family quickly and easily, then it might take one to two months. If they had moved around or moved overseas or for some reason he'd changed his name, it might be trickier to locate him. If he was not on the electoral roll, it could take a year or more.

Brenda advised that for a handful of their clients, they were unable to locate their families. If that happened, she assured us, there were ways and means that they might be able to try to give us more than Saul's first name. It would be a last resort, but it would allow us to do our own search. She asked us to bear with her; she would do her best to find him as soon as she could.

'If by chance you find out that he's deceased, what sort of information could we get then? Can we find out a bit more about his life?' Cynthia asked.

She said that not a lot of information would be released to us. However, if our mum applied, they'd be able to release more to her, including a copy of the birth certificate and a copy of the adoption order with his full adoptive name, his parents' names and where he lived.

'How long does Births, Deaths and Marriages take?' David asked.

Brenda hoped that it would be by the end of the following week, as long as he was in Victoria. She would ring or email me, and then I could let everyone know.

'So, if any of us have any other questions, we can ring you next week?' I asked.

Brenda assured us that we could call her anytime.

'We'll probably have to have another chat to Mum and Dad over the weekend and then possibly confirm with you on Monday if we're going ahead. It may be Cynthia, David, or me ringing you. Is that okay?' I asked.

Brenda said that was okay. She confirmed that she would email the court document to me so that we could take it with us when we chatted with our parents. There was no hurry on her end, or in terms of speaking to our folks. They might need time to think about things for a little while. She wished us well when we had the chat with our parents and said we must feel like the only family in the world that had been through this, but that we were not. She finished our conversation by saying that, however it turned out, we must look after each other.

Chapter 7

DEALING WITH THE FALLOUT

Psychoanalysis teaches one thing, he thought:
Nothing ever happens in a vacuum. A single bad act
can have all sorts of repercussions. —John Katzenbach[8]

AUGUST 2014

We were dealing with the fallout from our parents' choice to stay silent. I'm sure they didn't think about the negative consequences. Each of us would deal with it in our own ways, in our own time. We also had to consider our parents and how they would deal with it.

Certainly, the meeting with Brenda gave us more information to consider. Cynthia, David and I decided to meet with our parents to talk about what Brenda had told us. We could also give them a copy of the court document that Brenda emailed me. David decided he would ring Mum to ask her.

When David rang her, he was amazed at how eager she was to talk. He asked her if she wanted to meet and if our father also wanted to be involved. She told David that she would ask Dad if he wanted to join us, but she thought that he wouldn't want to. As we thought, Dad did not want to join the chat. Cynthia and David would pick Mum up from her house. They would then drive to meet me at the McDonald's near my work. It was supposed to be easy, but as I found out later, it went haywire pretty quickly.

When Cynthia and David arrived to pick up Mum, strangely, the house was locked up. They went to the front door and knew that Mum and Dad were inside, but Dad was not opening the door.

They could hear Mum saying, 'You need to let them in.'

After a moment, Dad went to the front door. He opened the door and let David pass to go inside.

'If you dare!' he said, as he stepped in front of Cynthia, his eyes black with fury.

After David entered, Dad closed and locked the door behind him.

Cynthia backed away from the front door, stunned. Her heart skipped a beat, and she began trembling as fear took hold. He was a very formidable man. This had never happened before, and she did not know what to do.

She went and sat in the car, scared, and she considered calling the police.

Luckily, Mum and David came outside soon after. Dad glared at Cynthia again. He tried to use standover tactics and instil fear. We had been scared in certain situations with him in the past, but this was completely unexpected.

We knew that he was fuming about our search for our brother. But why did he let David in the house and not Cynthia? Did he have something else to hide that we did not know about?

David and Mum joined Cynthia in the car, and they all drove away. Cynthia was happy to be away from the house, away from our father and his anger. But with the realisation of what had happened, she burst into tears.

Mum asked her why she was crying. Cynthia was unable to speak through her tears. David let Mum know what had happened. Mum said that she did not realise that Dad had acted that way. True to form, she defended our father and enabled his bad behaviour by saying he was angry that she'd broken the TV.

I could understand my mother defending him. I had been in a marriage where I had defended my first husband, a controlling and demanding man, much like my father. In this instance, though, my father's behaviour was unacceptable.

There had to be more to this than a broken TV—much more! And Cynthia was the one to pay for his anger that day. That was not fair.

Cynthia was so upset by what had happened that she couldn't be present with Mum, David and me for our chat. Instead, she rang Angus to ask him to pick her up and take her to our place. After her husband Billie finished work, he picked her up.

I met Mum and David at Macca's after work. I had no idea what had happened until I asked why Cynthia was not there. I was horrified when David told me. After I got over my initial shock and anger, we started talking. I knew we wouldn't get another opportunity to talk to mum if we didn't talk then—our dad would see to that.

We filled Mum in on everything Brenda had told us, including that her son's name was Saul. It must have felt good for her to know that, finally.

In our conversation, we told her that Brenda could start the search with Births, Deaths and Marriages. Brenda also advised us that Saul had not put a DNC in his records, meaning that if we found him, he could potentially be open to contact. Ultimately, it would be his choice to have contact with us or not.

We told our Mum that the five of us had unanimously decided that we wanted to continue with the search for Saul. We asked her if she wanted to be a part of it. She told us that she did not, although she was happy to know the outcome.

❋

A couple of weeks later, I chatted with David over the phone. I had been trying to ring him. I didn't know that he didn't want to talk to our parents, and so he was screening his calls. He was so angry about what Dad had done by locking Cynthia out. I had never heard him so angry. He said, 'Dad needs to apologise to Cynthia.'

David wanted to talk to Dad seriously about what had happened. He pointed to past poor behaviour like when Dad would introduce Mum to someone else as 'Dragon' or 'Driftwood'—the same nickname he had given Lee, my half-sister. David also mentioned that he hated it when, as kids, Dad would say he had one asset, David, and four liabilities, Jennifer, Cynthia, Nancy and me. He said he had always felt bad for us, and that we must have hated it also.

It is true, it wasn't great to hear your father call you a liability and your mother and sister driftwood. He would cover it by saying it in a joking manner. But he also said, in other situations, that 'there's a lot of truth in gest.' It was different, though, when a joke was directed at him. He would be annoyed, and that rule of gest did not apply. He used to say, 'You can give it but not take it.' This applied to him more than anyone else.

I suggested to David that he tread carefully when chatting to our dad. 'If you go in hard with Dad, you will only get his back up,' I said. It was true that our dad didn't acknowledge when he did, or said, the wrong thing. Even when he should, he would not say sorry.

I also said to David that he should be proud of who he is and of the fact that he didn't treat his family that way. I hoped that helped him. I am unsure if he ever confronted our father. But would it have changed anything? After all, our dad is that leopard who didn't change his spots for anything or anyone.

I also took the time to reflect and question my father's actions. Was I eager to let the 'bad' dad get away with outbursts like that and not hold him accountable for his actions? Most likely. There were times when I chose to talk about these things and other times, I remained silent. As a thirteen-year-old, I did not talk to my dad for three days. I'm not even sure why that happened. To end the stand-off, I just started talking, and it was over with or forgotten. Maybe I made my point, maybe I didn't. I tried to pick my fights, and I wanted to believe my dad was respectable and lovable, and so I often let him off too easily.

My mother did not have the strength to stand up to him. Did I have the strength to stand up to him? Probably not. In later life, he was more temperamental than ever.

I thought it was all too late; he would not change. I did not think he would ever say sorry or be accountable for any of his actions. I certainly did not think he would apologise for treating Cynthia so dreadfully.

I thought about Saul. Did he want to come into a family with all of that? I suppose all families have baggage. I hoped Saul would be grateful for five siblings and not worry about all the other stuff.

As always, I tried to focus on the positive rather than the negative. And the fact that we now knew our brother's actual name made it all the more real. It gave me great reason to want to celebrate and sing it out loud.

I would often find myself wondering if I would meet him without knowing, while living my life. Every man that I came across whom I did not know, I would wonder if he could be my brother. I would ask them their name or look at their name badge if they had one, to see if their name was Saul. One thing I knew for sure: I was not prepared to give up. Having a limited amount of information about him only served to encourage me to find out more.

SEPTEMBER 2014

To seek some clarity, I decided I wanted to consult a clairvoyant. I went to see a lady called Anne.

Anne told me things about my work, home and my children. I listened even further when she picked up on the fact that I had come for another reason. I wanted to know if she could tell me information about my brother. I prompted her without giving too much away that I was interested in details about him. She quickly realised there was more to the story.

When Anne told me that there were two brothers, I was stunned. I then told her that I had not met him, or them, due to adoption. She said that one of the boys, she believed, may have passed away at a young age. I knew I'd be shattered if my adopted brother, or brothers, weren't alive.

She relayed that it was unclear if they were twins or of a similar age. Anne told me that the eldest brother had been raised as an only child by parents who often told him he was loved and wanted. She said they were not Christian and that his adoptive mother remained unwell, and he was worried about her. Finding his siblings would be good timing for him, and he'd like to have contact with us.

It felt good to know that our brother would be receptive to us contacting him, but I was sceptical that we had two adopted brothers. It couldn't be true; how could it?

Twice she said, 'Don't give up on your search. Whatever you do, do not give up.' She told me that we would find out by the end of the year and that it would make our brother's Christmas. Wow, Christmas was only a few months away. Thinking about that happening so soon was consuming yet exciting. What if?

Soon after that, I told my mother about what Anne told me. I asked her why she thought Anne would say that there were two brothers, not one.

She said she didn't know.

Chapter 8
FINDINGS

You can't hide from the truth; it has a way of
coming back to bite you on the bum.

Over the coming weeks, we received little information from Brenda. She was very busy and, as a result, our case experienced significant delays. Regardless, the initial stages normally took the longest.

We already knew that when any further information was available, we would be limited in what could be released to us as siblings. The limited information we were given up to that point included that Saul had been admitted to the babies' home on 16 February, at five days old. From there, he was discharged into the care of his adoptive parents on 30 March.

We learnt from Brenda that Saul did not live in Victoria, as his name was not on the Victorian electoral roll. He could be living anywhere. The chance that he lived in Queensland was small. Wherever he might be, it meant that the search had to be widened, and we'd have to wait longer.

Each state and territory has its own privacy and adoption legislation. The rules for accessing personal or adoption information can vary. There is the Commonwealth Privacy Act 1988[9], and states can rely on their own legislation. For instance, in Victoria, they rely on the Victoria's Adoption Act 1984[10]. Understanding all of this can be a minefield, but ultimately, it protects the privacy rights of Australians.

I rang my mother to let her know the little bit of information we had. She sounded very chirpy when I explained.

'Do you think because he's not in Victoria, he may not want you to find him?' she asked.

During this search, she had been trying either to put us off or suggest other possibilities, and this conversation was no exception. I believe it was her way of still protecting or defending our father. His stance on us finding our brother had not changed.

'No, he's probably just moved interstate, and we don't know if that was during his childhood or adulthood,' I replied. 'Anyway, it means that the search may take longer than we thought.'

My father must have been listening, as I heard him saying something to her in the background. 'Hang on a minute,' Mum said down the phone.

I could hear her telling him that I had rung to give her more information about Saul. She asked him if he wanted to talk to me.

Instead of answering her, he grabbed the phone from her and to me he said, 'Do you want to hear something funny? Margie is joining the gym!' Margie was an elderly relative.

No pleasantries, just jokes. He gave the phone back to mum. If he did not talk about our search, he could pretend that it was not happening.

Later in September, I received an email from Brenda. She let me know that she had not been able to locate Saul, but she believed that she may have located his adoptive mother. It was not normal to make first contact with the adoptive parents. Since Brenda had not found any other information, she would be willing to contact his mother by mail if we agreed to go ahead.

This was exciting! We were possibly getting closer to finding our brother. It was one of the many times when reality became overwhelming. The what-if questions started all over again, but now they focused on Saul's mother. What if she were contactable and decided not to pass on the information to Saul? I could empathise with her in this hypothetical—she would have a huge decision to make. For her, it would mean her world could change forever. Not to mention the world of her son.

What if she did pass on the information to Saul, and he did not want any part of it? We could be one of those families that did not find their family member. I would be devastated not to meet him.

My heart was racing just thinking about those scenarios and the fact that this could be another standstill. Regardless of my fears, we had a decision to make.

I could not keep this to myself. I knew that Cynthia, David and Nancy were on a weekend camping trip about one hour from Brisbane. Angus and I did not hesitate to drive there that evening. I should have rung Jennifer while we were driving to the campsite. Instead, I was so excited and overwhelmed. I talked continuously to Angus. I would call her at camp.

When we arrived at the campsite it was dark. As we were staying overnight, we left the caravan hooked up to the car, allowing us to set up in record time. We would drive home early in the morning for our family commitments.

The others had already started the campsite fire, which was warm and cozy, and glowing below the sky, brilliant with stars. I could hear the cows in the nearby fields mooing.

'I have news,' I said.

I told them what Brenda had said about the possibility of locating Saul's mother. Brenda had advised that she could send a letter, care of Saul's mother, but addressed to Saul. We were all curious to know how she had located his mother. We talked about the risks and that the process could take some time. All in all, we agreed we could be getting closer to finding our brother.

'So, do we take the leap and ask Brenda to send a letter?' I asked each of my siblings and Jennifer over the telephone.

Unanimously again, we all agreed. Even though it was a Sunday, I emailed Brenda as soon as I could after Angus, and I arrived home. I asked her to go ahead and send the letter. I asked Brenda to call me when she could.

Brenda called me the next day. I asked how she had managed to find Saul, or at least the address of his mother. It appeared that it was easier than we could have imagined. She said she found the address in a telephone book since his surname was not a common one. I realised that there was still a big chance it would not lead us to Saul's family.

Brenda reiterated that she would wait a couple of weeks after sending the letter to give Saul time to respond. If she did not hear anything, she would send another request by registered post.

Oh my goodness.

If only everything about our situation were that easy and conceivably lucky. We might have some answers within a couple of weeks. Even with those thoughts, I was not prepared to get my hopes up. But my nervousness was undeniable. What if this failed? I might sink back into the anger or mourning stage. I didn't want to think about that possibility.

OCTOBER 2014

Nineteen days later, the longest nineteen days ever, and we had a response. Brenda tried ringing me at work, but I was in the middle of an emergency with a patient. She told the receptionist she would send me an email. After I finished, I stole a few quiet minutes to duck into a corner and check my emails.

Brenda confirmed that she had spoken over the phone with Saul!

I looked away, wiping my eyes and re-reading the words. Goosebumps cloaked me from head to toe. A big smile spread across my face. I felt light with relief and disbelief. I didn't know whether to laugh, dance or cry. With a surge of adrenaline and energy, I jumped up and down. This was what we wanted; my world had just become brighter.

We had started this search in June, and by October, we had news that our brother had contacted Brenda. I was eternally grateful to her at that moment.

For the rest of my shift, I went about my tasks without really thinking. Muscle memory took over, my mind consumed with thoughts of our brother. After work, I read the email for the third time, this time comprehending the impact.

I could not keep this news to myself. After arriving home that evening, I let my four siblings know.

'Brenda has spoken to Saul!' I blurted out when I spoke to them.

They were shocked. I told them everything that I learnt from Brenda's email. Including that Saul was, quite understandably, overwhelmed, but also very receptive. She wrote that, thankfully, he'd always known he was adopted, and he listened intently as Brenda told him about us. He had always thought this day might come.

When Brenda told him that we are, as far as we know, full siblings, he agreed to have contact, initially by email. She wrote that Saul is eager and positive and that he's looking forward to contacting. After everything, I still did not believe that this was happening. It was something I'd been dreaming about for the last few months, but now it was happening.

After we all chatted, I emailed Brenda, thanking her for the fantastic news about Saul wanting to have contact. I told her how excited we were and how I had jumped up and down after reading her email. Knowing how we felt, I couldn't imagine how Saul must have felt.

That night, I slept like a baby. It may have been the celebratory drink I had earlier that evening, but most likely it was the knowledge that we had found our brother!

Chapter 9

FIRST ENCOUNTERS

*Our first meeting was like a page turning in the
book of my life, forever marking the beginning
of an incredible journey.* —Anonymous

Brenda emailed me with Saul's email address. Previously, during our chat with Brenda, she suggested that one person, probably me, email Saul first, as all of us would be too overwhelming. But what could I write to my brother whom I had never met?

It didn't take me long to get the courage up to start writing. I deleted, added and changed the words over and over again until it all became a blur. Finally, I settled on what I was going to write. The very first email I sent to my brother was sent on Thursday 16 October 2014.

Hi Saul,

My name is Chris. I am your sister! This is not an email I ever thought I would be writing, but on so many fronts, it is truly amazing. We found out about you in May this year, and as a united sibling front, we decided to search for you immediately, unaware of the outcome, of course. I am delighted to be sending this email, which is also on behalf of all of us.

I just would like to say a very big thank you to your Mum for passing on the information. She must be an amazing lady.

Brenda has let me know what she told you about us. To let you know a little bit more about us, there are five of us [...].

This has been awesome for us, but it must be extremely overwhelming for you. We are very mindful of that. Of course, we understand you must have so many questions as we do about you. For instance, the area you live in and what kind of work you do. But we will be guided by the steps you want or the questions you want answered and to answer. We look forward to hearing from you soon with any information you may wish.

Cheers,

Chris

I hoped I hadn't bombarded him with information. I had included details about the five of us, our families and what we did for work.

I checked my emails at every chance I could that day. I had no idea when Saul would read my email. Would he be checking for my response, like I was checking for his? Would he email me back straight away? Or would he need to think about it first? I had no idea how he would react. I tried to be patient and wait.

Thankfully, I didn't have to wait long. Saul must have been as eager as I was, as he replied to my email at 7:43 pm that evening.

Hey Chris,

Wow! I have no words!

I'll find some.

Truly wonderful, yes, I have many questions.

Don't know where to start, I'm Saul [...] on Facebook, not sure if you are on or not.

I would love to chat on Messenger, if that's not too soon for you, maybe some other chat if you prefer. Emails can be long-winded.

I'm so happy to have received your email and am very much looking forward to talking and meeting you all. I hope this is where we are heading, as soon as possible for me.

With love

Saul

Saul's email revealed more details about him and his sense of humour as he confirmed he was, in fact, 'a boy'.

I read and re-read his email, in particular, 'with love.' Wow, that was out of this world! Then I thought about him wanting to talk and meet us all, 'as soon as possible.' Was this really happening?

Before I knew it, a telephone conversation was arranged between Saul and me for two days later, on Saturday.

On Saturday, Saul sent me a text message to ask if he could call before lunch. I was eager to talk, and I didn't want to miss his call, so I told him that I was free then.

'Thanks,' he replied, 'I'll call in five.'

I jumped up and down on the spot, nervous with anticipation. I was not one for outwardly showing my excitement by jumping. As usual, though, my hands were sweaty, and my heart was beating so fast. I paced around the house.

'What do I say? I don't know what to say!' I told Angus.

He said, 'Just be yourself.'

I watched the clock intently. He would be calling in four minutes. Time seemed to stand still. What if he didn't call? It could have been a monumental mistake or a joke on me.

My phone sat on the kitchen bench. I stared at it, willing it to ring. After what seemed like hours, the chime-like ring beckoned me. I lunged across the bench and grabbed my phone before it fell silent.

'Hello!'

'Chris?'

'Yes, Saul? Oh my goodness, I don't believe it is you,' I said, giving myself a bit of time to think about what I wanted to say.

I walked outside and started walking around the side of our house along the concrete driveway. I always like to walk when talking on the phone.

'Yes, it's me,' he said.

I tried to listen to the sound of his voice, even with the few words I had to go by. Did he sound like anyone from the family?

Somehow, the words popped out of my mouth, and I said, 'I didn't think this would ever happen. I have to say, when we started this, I didn't think you would want to know us. I am so glad you do ... Sorry if I am rambling a little bit here.'

'Yes, so am I,' he said, sounding a bit emotional. 'I don't know what to say or how to do this.'

'Don't worry, that makes two of us,' I said and paused. 'So, have you always known that you are adopted?' I continued, as the questions sprang into my mind.

'Yes, from as long as I can remember. I will tell you a bit about my family,' he said. 'My mum and dad had a daughter naturally. Then my mum had a few miscarriages, so they decided to take me on board. That was four years later, then three years after that, they decided to take on another boy.'

We talked for an hour and six minutes, not that I was counting. During that time, he explained that his family had moved from Melbourne when he was seven years old to Currumbin in Queensland.

His dad worked at Currumbin Wildlife Sanctuary until he retired. He passed away in 1996. He said that he had good contact with his mother and sister.

Saul spoke about his work life, as a tiler—work that he loved. But he found that the work had become too physically demanding, which led him to seek another career. At the time, he lived in north Queensland, but he felt that it was time for a change. In his personal life, he did not have children; he had married young, but that marriage broke down. He had recently reconnected through Facebook with an old flame, Tillie, from his teen years.

I told him about how we moved around a lot to different homes and towns in Victoria. He asked if I was born in Geelong. I told him that all five of us were born in Geelong. I said that we'd moved around Victoria and when I was fifteen we left Victoria before settling in Queensland nine months later. During our chat, we realised that we would have been living in the same areas at the same time. We may have walked past each other on the beach or in the shops, and we did not even know how much of a connection we had. My maternal grandparents loved Currumbin Wildlife Sanctuary and would often visit. They may have walked past or even seen Saul's dad whilst he was working one day. My grandparents have lived in the Tweed Shire area since the late 1980s.

I talked to Saul about us settling in Brisbane when I was 16 in grade 11, and that I have been living in the area ever since. I then spoke about my relationships and my children. Mum and Dad came up in the conversation.

Saul said, 'I get the impression your mum's controlled.'

I said, 'Yes. And what I will say about dad is that he's very old school.'

I was amazed that we talked for so long on our first conversation. Aside from the initial nervousness and the hesitation about what to talk about, once we got started, there weren't any pauses or uncomfortable silences. It felt as though, in that moment, we had known each other so much longer than just one phone conversation. Incredible.

＊

Everything began moving so quickly then. Especially when Saul decided to come and meet us in person. We only found out about him a few months before, then I spoke to him on the phone and now suddenly we were going to meet on the Gold Coast.

Saul and his partner, Tillie, would fly in from north Queensland. Jennifer arranged to fly up from Sydney. Cynthia, David, Nancy and I and our families decided to camp in one of the Gold Coast caravan parks we liked.

David decided he would like to meet Saul in person first, since they had arrived before everyone else. I thought it was a good idea. He had grown up with only sisters; now it was his time to meet our brother. His brother. I did not begrudge him that experience, even if I felt a little envious.

David kept us up to date with text messages throughout their meeting that evening.

'All going well! He's a top bloke!'

David sent a photo of the two of them. I was looking at the first photo of my brother. They stood closely together, happy smiles on their faces. I noticed that Saul was taller than David. David had blondish wavy hair, and Saul had darker, curlier hair.

Looking at the photo of Saul brought up a deep twinge of bottled-up resentment for our parents. They had kept us apart. We had missed possibly half of our lives not knowing each other; that was a huge thing to be taken away from us. But they could no longer keep us apart.

I could only imagine how Saul might have been feeling. He had just discovered that his birth family was large, with five direct siblings. That had to be daunting and massive for him.

I hoped that we all liked each other. We had not been siblings before now, as such, but we could be siblings and friends from here on in. I was crossing all my fingers and toes that our meeting could be the start of many fond memories together.

NOVEMBER 2014

Saturday, 1 November 2014, was our Meet Day. We had arranged to meet at 3:00 pm, in the apartment where Saul and his partner Tillie were staying. It was raining heavily as if the heavens wept for what we had lost. Despite the rain, my mood could not be dampened.

I texted him in the morning, 'Hi Saul, today is the day! Amazing!' I was enthusiastic and eager to meet him.

'Sounds good, butterflies here too!' he texted back.

Saul told me that his adoptive mother had expressed interest in meeting us. He wanted to know if we were okay with that. I let him know that we would love to meet her. I was excited to find out more about him from his mother. I hoped that she would tell us stories about his childhood that only a mother can tell.

Saul let his mother know that it was okay to come along and meet us.

He wrote to me that she'd texted him back saying she had, 'Bats, not butterflies lol.' She may have been feeling overwhelming dread and nerves for something that she thought might come one day. I imagine her heart would have been heavy as she was about to meet her son's biological family. That would be a huge deal, which could be unsettling for her.

Just before 3:00 pm, the five of us siblings travelled in Cynthia's car to Saul and Tillie's unit. Our families and partners remained at the caravan park; we didn't want to overwhelm Saul with all of us at the first meeting. I wondered what we would talk about and whether the conversation would be easy.

Saul must have been watching out for us as he met us as soon as the car pulled into the car park. I suddenly was covered in goosebumps, and I felt butterflies in my stomach. I could feel tears of joy run down my cheeks as he walked towards us. We said hello, and then he gave me the biggest and most embracing hug ever! I felt warm, cozy and completely safe, and any doubt melted away. It was almost like I could feel the uncertainty and mental anguish of the past few weeks and months drift away.

I forgot to breathe. I inhaled deeply, bringing myself back to the present moment. I managed a squeaky, 'Hi.'

One by one, Saul gave us all huge enveloping hugs. We then followed him in silence up the stairs and into the unit where Tillie and his mum waited patiently. I walked over to his mum and kissed her on the cheek. I called her Mum, as weird as it seems—a habit I had acquired from work.

One by one, we introduced ourselves. Tillie said, 'Oh, so many girls.'

I later found out that Tillie was also an adoptee, and she had had some contact with her biological family.

Saul offered us all a drink. We kindly declined before sitting in the lounge room on the floor in a circle formation. It was almost like we were sitting on the mat in primary school, waiting for the teacher to read a book. Instead of anyone speaking, we all looked at each other in silence.

Cynthia and Tillie spoke about starting the conversation with a get-to-know-you game to break the ice. It would have been one of those games that you play on the first day of school. The stillness remained.

Saul eventually decided to break the ice by saying, 'Thank you all for coming.'

'No, thank you, this is really incredible,' I said. 'When we started this journey looking for you, we didn't know what would happen. In so many situations like this, the adoptee does not want to know the biological family ...' I paused, feeling more tears, 'and we really didn't know if you would want to know us, so, thank you.'

'I know exactly what you mean, it's okay,' Saul's mum said.

I smiled at her. I hoped that someone else would say something, but no one did. Awkwardness lingered. The sweatiness returned to my hands for the second time. It was so awkward and overwhelming. No one knew what to say. Even the small talk was not forthcoming.

The silence almost bounced off the walls. David walked onto the balcony of the unit for a moment of fresh air. Even though he had already met Saul, I could tell that he was uncomfortable and unsure what to say.

In a bid to break the tone, I blurted out without thinking that it would put Saul on the spot, 'Maybe you could tell us about yourself, Saul.'

At that moment, I felt very inept and tongue-tied. I thought that after the initial uncomfortable moment, the conversation would flow, much like our telephone chat. Instead, it was like I was in a maze with towering, hedged walls, narrow walkways and a never-ending path, desperately looking for an escape. I felt like I wanted to be swallowed up into the hedge to avoid the awkwardness.

Saul suggested that we go over the road to the surf club. Great idea, I thought. If we remove ourselves from that moment, from within our heads and our nervousness, maybe the conversation would flow more easily.

It was raining when we stepped out of the unit. It could have been torrential rain, and we still would have walked to the surf club just for a change of scenery. We were all seeking a calm place to get to know each other, and maybe the surf club was going to be that place.

Once outside, Jennifer and Saul's mum walked on ahead, talking like they had known each other for years. Saul and Tillie pulled away from the group to have a cigarette.

Inside the surf club, it was noisy but inviting, a complete contrast to the four walls of the unit, where you could hear a pin drop. Conveniently, like fate had made a reservation, there was a table for the eight of us. The change of environment was a game-changer. We must have all found our voices in the walk across the road.

Saul's mum talked a lot, which helped to break the ice. She told us that they had spent holidays on the Gold Coast when Saul was little. They loved the coastal areas and the days they spent on the beach with the children when they were younger. On one of those holidays, Saul's dad, who had passed away about 20 years earlier, suggested that they move to Queensland. When they moved, they left all of their family in Melbourne, not knowing anyone. Saul was seven.

The rest of the afternoon continued well. We were especially thankful to Saul's mother for joining us. Not only was she a dynamic, funny, loving lady, but we were so glad to meet her. Her spirited conversation was just what we all needed to break the ice, allowing us to enjoy the moment.

After dinner that night, Saul and Tillie joined us at the caravan park. With the initial meeting done, the second meeting was less intense. Saul and Tillie met most of our partners and children that evening. I'm sure that would have been a lot for them to take in, let alone remembering the names.

That night, at times, I would have to stop myself from staring, but I could not help it. If I were noticed, I would turn my eyes in another direction. My daughter sometimes pulls me back from staring at people. But really, I don't stare—I people-watch. So, I'd peek another look whenever I could. I was trying to see who Saul looked like and, when he spoke, who he sounded like.

I thought he was his own person physically, but he reminded me of my mother's family. His voice reminded me of my cousins—my dad's twin brothers' sons. Saul seemed very laidback and casual.

I could tell that Saul also watched quietly. He was sitting back in his camp chair and watching us, his biological family, for the first time. He seemed to be absorbing and processing who we were and how we all fitted within the family dynamics. He could have been looking to decipher who might look or behave like him or vice versa.

The next day, we would meet again. We remembered to capture the moment with some photos of the now six siblings. I have that photo on my buffet at home with Saul, me, Jennifer, Cynthia, David and Nancy standing in order of our age. Amusing, I realised. Saul also obliged by getting photos with some of his new nieces and nephews. After all, he was now part of a big biological family.

But did he want to be part of this family? Did he really want five siblings?

Chapter 10
MOVING FORWARD

*Life is like riding a bicycle. To keep you balance,
you must keep moving.* —Albert Einstein

Moving forward was a strange feeling. When I sat with my brother, even though we shared a birthright, he was a stranger to me. I should know him so well, and yet I did not. That part of our journey had only just begun.

We were originally five siblings who had known each other since birth, the way it's meant to be. The five of us knew each other's ways, imperfections and idiosyncrasies. We had grown close over the years, particularly during adulthood. It was undeniable that if we needed to be there for each other, we would do our darndest.

But now we were six, not five. How would things change within our family dynamics? What would follow? I wondered about the memories we could create to look back on in the future. As our full-blooded brother, I hoped the moments and the memories would now be limitless and lifelong.

Individually and together, we all had the opportunity to get to know Saul, and he got to know us in return. Our parents also decided to come on board and meet Saul. We had done all the hard work; we had determined that Saul was not 'in jail,' as my father had initially insinuated. My parents deserved to meet him. Their meeting with Saul would turn out to be the only time our father met Saul.

David had asked Tillie on that first night camping on the Gold Coast if she thought that Saul would like to meet our parents. When Saul agreed, David arranged a meeting on another day.

It felt idiosyncratic that when Saul talked about his adoptive family, he referred to his adoption as 'coming on board.' Similarly, I used the same phrase above when describing my parents' decision to meet him. Maybe it's just an Aussie way of talking, or a similarity to each other's way of speaking, that I had not noticed until now. It could be that I'm still looking for ways to confirm that we are alike; that I am my brother's sister.

Anyway, Saul and our parents met for the first time on the Gold Coast. It took a lot to impress our father, but he was impressed by Saul. After their initial meeting, he went to the extent of writing a letter to Saul's adoptive mother. He thanked her for the great job she had done raising Saul.

My father writing a letter to anyone was a big thing. As far as I know, he only ever wrote one or two letters in his lifetime.

Since we met Saul, he had moved from north Queensland to country New South Wales, and then back to southern Queensland. Now that he's closer, it's much easier for all of us to see each other. I think he may have inherited the family trait of moving around. But I don't think Saul was running, like our parents may have been.

No matter where he lived, we got to know Saul over the next few years. We finally had the chance for him to come to our family celebrations and for us to go to his. Whenever he was in town, we would catch up. We'd all missed out on so many other celebrations over the years.

Celebrating weddings was a big one for me. We missed his wedding and he missed ours. My first marriage collapsed. To me, marriage is a sacred thing, only broken when all else completely fails. When I chose to leave my first marriage, aside from how it would affect my children, I felt the failure deeply.

I did not think I would meet another, but against all odds, and after seven years of being together with Angus, I got married a second time. As a definite on the guest list, Saul and Tillie came to our wedding in 2016. That was such a momentous occasion for me. I was marrying the man who had shown me how to love and live life like never before. We chose to do it our way, right down to making the bouquets and organising a sand ceremony.

Our five kids stood with us at the altar: Angus's son stood by him, next to my youngest son. Our two girls walked down the aisle before me, and then together they beautifully played the song, 'A Thousand Years', on the piano as my eldest son proudly walked me down the aisle. I looked directly at Angus—my awesome husband, soon to be—then at our children and guests, and my smile would have said a thousand words. It was hard to stop the tears of joy in my eyes, as I soaked up the moment with our amazing children by our side. A truly special, beautiful and unforgettable moment that I cherish.

A sand ceremony, or Unity Sand Ceremony, is a tradition used where the bride and groom pour sand from a separate vase into a unified central vase or container. We chose to follow this tradition as a way of symbolising our union and our separate families coming together. The seven of us poured our favourite-coloured sand into the central vase, unifying our marriage and our blended family.

We got married at a resort on the Gold Coast that had a chapel and a reception room, about an hour or so from home. All of us, guests included, stayed in the accommodation for the weekend. The festivities started with drinks on Friday night, then our wedding the next day, followed by breakfast on Sunday morning. It was a full weekend of celebrations. Not only did I marry my love that day, but it was a magical, amazing day and weekend that brought family and friends together. I cherished the moment even more with Saul and Tillie there to celebrate with us.

After our big day, Angus and I had a couple of days, gifted by my work, in the Sunshine Coast Hinterland for our honeymoon. We stayed in a charming treetop bungalow that overlooked the picturesque views of stunning, lush foliage. One of my favourite places and things to do is to spend time in the beauty of nature. We spent a beautiful, glorious couple of days and nights, just the two of us, as husband and wife.

The second part of our honeymoon was camping on the beach. I am unable to choose between the beauty of the beach and the serenity of the bush. Both hold a special place for me, in different ways. This part of our honeymoon was special, as the kids joined us, and some of my siblings and their families, including Saul and Tillie.

Our complete honeymoon should have been for the two of us; that is true. But when Saul suggested going camping, I was not going to miss out on that. We had only known Saul as our brother for about eighteen months at that stage. I would take any opportunity to spend time with him, even at the end of our honeymoon.

During this beach camping expedition, we met Saul's sister, Rita and her husband Mark for the first time. Rita was the biological child born to Saul's adoptive parents. Whilst camping all together that weekend, we made great connections and emphasised that we were all family now.

Earlier in 2025, Angus and I camped again with Saul and Tillie, Rita and Mark, and a friend of Tillie's called Angie. Rita and I bonded so much on that weekend. She told me about how, when we met while camping at the end of my honeymoon, she was nervous meeting us. Rita, an outwardly strong and wonderful lady, had hidden her apprehension very well. I said that back then, and now, she should not be worried. We are family after all.

During our honeymoon camping trip, we drove in convoy along the beach and explored the coastline. I was a little nervous about beach driving, but in the end, I loved it. Saul bought his paddleboards with him. At Rainbow Beach, adults and teenagers alike tried to catch a ride with the small waves.

If I want to do something, despite any odds, I will stick with it until I get it. That day was no exception. I kept trying over and over again to stand on the paddleboard. Finally, I surfed on a small wave almost to the water's edge—I stood tall, with my arms outstretched, a wide, melancholy smile on my lips. It may not have been a big wave, but I did it. Yes!

At mealtimes, we all ate and socialised in our mess-hut. Often, we were joined by kangaroos. I guess they were used to campers who had fed them before, or maybe they'd learned to scurry after human food. We did not encourage or feed them.

Large goannas also liked to follow us around. Not having much contact in the past with goannas, I was pretty scared. On one occasion, it appeared like a very large goanna was following me. Every time I tried to turn in another direction, it would head towards me. When it ran straight for me, I yelled out to Angus. He managed to steer the goanna in another direction.

For another reason, being with family during the latter part of our honeymoon was just what we needed. We possibly should have stayed at home, as sadly, we were also grieving for a very close friend. He was one of Angus's closest friends; they had known each other all of their adult lives. I had known him since 2001, and he was Godfather to my youngest son.

He had been instrumental in Angus and me getting together. I will never forget the proud look on his face when Angus and I married. Then, a couple of days later, he was taken too soon and without warning. A week later, we attended his funeral. We will always be grateful that we knew him and that he was a friend to all seven of us. We will always remember and miss him.

Saul and Tillie came to Angus's 50th birthday in 2017. The night sky was aglow with bright, shiny stars as we celebrated with a BBQ in our backyard. Angus wanted a reggae-themed evening with everyone coming dressed in Rastafarian clothes. We played reggae music, ate fabulous salads and BBQ meats and shared meaningful conversations and laughter over a drink or two. It was an awesome way for Angus to celebrate his birthday with family and friends. For me, it was extra special with Saul and Tillie there.

The celebrations did not end there. To make up for our 'shared' honeymoon, my gift to Angus for his birthday included two tickets on a cruise to Hamilton Island. Neither of us had been on a cruise. Aside from my foot being supported in a Moonboot due to an accident and a bout of motion sickness on the last evening, we had an amazing holiday.

We all celebrated with another camping trip for Saul's 50th birthday. It was the first birthday celebration that we would all spend together. All of us—Cynthia, David, Nancy, myself and our partners, as well as Rita and Mark—all camped with Saul and Tillie in northern New South Wales. It was another great weekend of celebrations and solidifying the foundations of our family.

Camping quickly became a fun group activity that we all enjoyed.

Going to concerts soon became another. Two years ago, we all, including Rita and Mark, came together for a concert and stayed at Saul and Tillie's home. We let our hair down, around the fire that Saul built in the backyard, with good food and great company. At the concert, we all danced and partied to the music of different artists. It was another fun weekend of not letting the chance go by to create more memories together.

When I look back now, especially, since we had not long met, we crammed in a lot by taking every opportunity we could to spend time together as family. We would steal a few moments, no matter how big or small. Stealing time is a funny way to put it, but really, we did not want to forfeit such opportunities, for those times were our moments to get to know each other.

There was even a time when Saul came to Brisbane for medical reasons. We met him for dinner. The next day, I stole more time to spend with him before he boarded a plane to fly home. Sneaking about an hour of chatting after driving through heavy traffic to the airport was so worth it.

As we chatted, a friend of Saul's noticed him and stopped to say hello. It appeared that he was also flying home that afternoon, but on a different flight. What happened next, I did not expect. Saul introduced me to his friend as his sister. It was an amazing moment. I thought, I really am his sister! I still have to pinch myself sometimes when I think that I have an older brother, especially when he refers to me as his sister.

My mum got to meet Saul's sister Rita on one occasion. Saul and Tillie were staying near Currumbin Wildlife Sanctuary, and we all joined them, including Mum, for a BBQ dinner. For my mum, it was a nice evening to spend time with Saul and for her to meet Rita in person.

Saul and Tillie were not staying in the same unit that they stayed in when we met for the first time a few years earlier. But for me, staying so close put me in a very nostalgic mood. How far we had come. When I looked back at our relationships over those first five years, it was remarkable.

Not everything was easy, though. I realised that while we spent a lot of time at gatherings, we spent more time talking over the phone. The phone gave me a place where I could feel most comfortable. Ridiculous though it sounds, I could talk more freely about anything and everything with Saul at the end of our phones.

I had taken myself back to our first conversation on the phone, which was easy and flowing, as opposed to our first in-person meeting, which was quiet and uncertain. Hiding behind the phone, I could converse easily, but in person, I was more vulnerable and found it much harder.

What also contributed to my sense of not knowing what to say or simply being myself around Saul was my past feelings of being a nervous introvert, with low self-esteem. In the past, especially in groups, I found it hard to start or even take part in conversations. What could I say without sounding boring, dull or dreary? Not only that, but I do not have a loud voice, and so other voices would be heard above mine whenever I did speak. Later, I would ridicule myself for not speaking up.

It's not like I don't have the words to say; I can write all these words here. It's easy to hide behind a keyboard and write the words, that is true. But it was the nervousness and my past insecurities coming back to haunt me.

It was then that I started to learn and work hard at expressing myself louder, in groups, at times. I've learnt that language has power when I am true, clear and myself. I realised that I deserved to treat myself better, in a way that I treat others. I, too, have things to say that may interest others. I may have lived behind a shield, but this part of my journey in life has taught me to be true to myself.

Becoming a meditation teacher, writing my own meditation scripts and seeing the smiles and the relaxed state of being for those who have attended my sessions has helped. Just knowing that I have helped another person has helped me in amazing ways. Angus and my siblings have also been instrumental in my believing in myself. After my first date with Angus, he bought me a plaque that said, 'Do what you love—CHASE YOUR DREAMS!' For Christmas last year, he bought me a coffee cup that simply said— 'Believe.'

I have learnt to let go of my fear and shine. My world has opened up a lot since letting go of that, so I can be the real me and be rid of those low self-esteem issues, which is great.

I realised that I was doing the same thing to myself when I met Saul and didn't allow myself to be me. I had reverted backwards. Not all the time, just sometimes. I do not know what made me start doing this. Maybe as I got to know him, I started thinking about things too much, or I could have been scared that he was not going to like me as his sister.

Whatever the reasoning, I had to stop. I'd let go of it in the past; now I had to do it again. I had to work to allow myself to be me around my brother.

I had to let go and accept that I had not grown up with Saul. It still saddens me today that we did not grow up together as brother and sister. Yet, that was not of our doing. I could not and did not control that. But we do have the rest of our lives. I had to be grateful for that.

This would become clear whenever I reread my journal entries from those times. One day, I was reading them at my youngest son's tennis lesson. I hoped that none of the other parents noticed me wiping away my tears. Even as I read my words, and then wrote them here, my eyes would well up with tears for the tragedy that would have befallen us all if we hadn't found our brother.

FEBRUARY 2020

Angus and I decided to go on a road trip along the eastern states of Australia. He had not been to Victoria, and his lifelong wish was to travel the Great Ocean Road.

I had not been home to Victoria for a visit in a very long time, either. I remember my siblings and I agreeing that Victoria would always be our home when we left. Honestly, though, the warmth and the sunshine of Queensland have been way too alluring. I had been back for funerals, sadly, but not for a holiday.

We decided we would travel by road to Victoria from Queensland. The entire trip was no easy feat, especially since we stayed in one location for each of the fifteen nights we were away.

We left home early on Valentine's Day. The kids, who were young adults by then, looked after the house, including our pet dog and chickens. We stayed with family and friends from night to night. I had not seen some of them for many years. It was awesome to see them and catch up. We also had dinner with my beautiful school friends in Benalla. We talked as if I had not left years earlier, as a fifteen-year-old. We laughed and giggled about old times until the venue we were at wanted to close the doors. We had the best time reconnecting.

We did manage to drive along the Great Ocean Road. We were told that it would be quiet in the region, as that thing called COVID-19 was keeping tourists away. The tourist venues may have been subdued, but a lot of the accommodation venues did not have vacancies. Luckily, we found the last room available. We arrived at 9:00 pm and located the key in the overnight box. The local pizza shop thankfully was still open.

The little things like this, as well as catching up with family and friends, made this a special and sometimes unusual holiday.

On the way home, we stayed with Saul and Tillie. They had moved from Queensland to New South Wales by then. It felt weird that I had not stayed at my own brother's home until then. It is something I took for granted with my other siblings. Another opportunity that I would not have missed.

When we arrived, Saul was working hard shovelling soil out the front of his steep driveway. He was a hard worker, much like the rest of us. He stopped, greeted us and showed us around his amazing home. Their décor was eclectic and I loved it.

That night, he showed me some photos of himself as a kid. Luckily, I was not being self-conscious or my introverted self, and we stayed up until all hours talking and laughing. Angus took a photo of Saul and me, laughing like kids. He was wearing the cap that I had given him for his 50th birthday that said, 'Grey Nomad.' I gave it to him as a joke because he was older than me. I would often joke with him that he was now the oldest, that he had to take the reins—so to speak.

Unfortunately, we had to go home the next day. Luckily, we did, as we made it just in time before the world changed forever.

I was very used to change in my world. We had found our brother, and then the pandemic changed the world for everyone. Our mindsets and outlook on life changed so quickly.

Angus and I were so grateful for our holiday, and I was thankful to have spent just one night in Saul's home. The next year or so was mostly phone contact only, of course.

In February 2023, Angus and I started what I hoped to be a new tradition with Saul. We went and spent another night at Saul and Tillie's home for our birthdays, since he'd moved back to South East Queensland. Both mine and Saul's birthdays fall in the same month, just ten days apart. Unlike Saul's 50th with the whole family, it was just going to be Angus and me sharing the time with Saul and Tillie.

Each occasion that I shared with my brother seemed surreal. I have learnt to leave behind the hurt and anger caused by my parents' actions, and to enjoy our time together and have fun. I could dwell on the fact that we only found out about Saul when we were in our forties. I often wonder, if we had met in our twenties, would we have had the same relationship that we have now? I doubt it.

I was married to my first husband at twenty-four, and I had my first child at twenty-seven. I was busy raising three children and building my own life, the good and the bad of it. My first husband was very controlling of my time, and he would not have wanted me to devote my time to another of my siblings.

Sometimes in life, things happen for a reason and in their own time. Maybe this was one of those things that happened when, how and where it was meant to.

We all sometimes take things for granted and let opportunities slip through our fingers. Right from the beginning, we did not want to let this slip through our fingers. All of the experiences, moments and opportunities with my brother were not taken for granted, not once, not ever. I am so grateful that our brother wanted to meet us and that he wanted to get to know us. We were given the chance to build a great relationship as brother and sister, the way it should have been.

Without the initial conversation and the questions raised by my Aunty Lisa, we would probably never have known that Saul was out there. I am grateful to her for letting us know that part of our history that we had no idea about. Angus and our children were amazing throughout that journey. They have adapted well to the fact that I have another brother, and that they have another brother-in-law or another uncle.

Now we can all look toward the next umpteen years ahead as a family, which thankfully also includes Saul, Tillie, Rita and Mark. They say that you can't choose your family, but you choose your friends. Well, I choose both my family and my friends. I certainly chose Saul as an amazing part of that.

When I look back on our journey, from the moment when I fully realised that I really am his sister, to now, I can see that we have come a long way. It has been a journey of letting go of some parts of the past, with tears, laughter and getting to know each other's quirks and ways. We may have been raised in different families, but we had finally become family, like we were meant to be.

For that, I will be forever grateful.

MORE TO DISCOVER

Chapter 11
NOT AGAIN

The best way out is always through. —Robert Frost[11]

You cannot protect yourself from sadness without protecting yourself from happiness. —Jonathan Safran Foer[12]

2017

In the morning of 22 June 2017, I rang my mother to see if she wanted me to take her to the hospital to visit my father. I had the day off, and she didn't drive. It would not be an ordinary hospital visit. My father's health was failing quickly, and we didn't know. I'm unsure if the doctors rang my mum to advise her of his condition. But even if they had, did she understand, or did she choose not to pass that information on? Maybe she didn't realise how bad it was.

When we walked into his room, I noticed that he was not conscious. He lay still in his bed, only grimacing or moaning a little at times. The nurse gave him more morphine, which helped to settle him. I asked her if he was dying, and she said she did not think so. But to me, his breath was slow with long gaps. I touched his skin; it was cold and pale. I knew that he was dying.

A little while after the nurse left the room, I said to my mother that he was going. Believing that hearing is the last of our senses to fade as we are dying, I suggested she talk to him and say it's okay for him to go. Her words were perfect. The last thing I said to him was that we would look after Mum.

While she spoke, I tuned out as I looked at the ceiling. I did that a lot in my father's presence. I was pointlessly looking for a sign that he had passed away, but of course, I did not get that sign from the ceiling. Confirmation came to me when I looked at his eyes, and I knew then.

I walked out of the room to find a nurse. I was completely calm when the nurse confirmed that he had passed. I left the room so my mum could sit with him.

It was then that David arrived. I told him that Dad had gone, and I asked him if he wanted to go into the room. He did not want to; he wanted to deal with the sudden news in his own way. He was the closest of all of us to him.

I rang my other siblings, including Saul, and told them matter-of-factly that he had gone. I did not cry.

Two weeks before, Cynthia, David and I had flown down to Victoria for the funeral of our father's identical twin. We knew that our uncle had been seriously ill before his passing, whereas we did not know that my father was critically unwell. I was sad and cried at my uncle's funeral.

The day of my father's funeral was surreal. My siblings and I did not want to give a eulogy. My dad was the last of his siblings to pass, and so our mother's brother kindly did it instead. It was nicely written. To my surprise, his funeral was attended by a lot more people than I had expected. Many actually liked him.

I don't remember shedding a lot of tears for him on the day of his passing, his funeral or after. We all had to deal with our part in his life, be it good or bad. I wish that things had been different. In our lifetimes, we will all have regrets, which is unavoidable, but it is the level of regret that is important. I did not have a great relationship with him, especially in later years. I genuinely wanted to have a good dad. That was the sad part.

I know he did the best he could. As I stated above, he was not the dad that I wanted. But maybe his trauma was too great for him to be the man or the father that he could have been. I will never know the answers to that.

After his funeral, I wished him peace and to finally be at rest.

JUNE 2019

We did look after Mum, as I said to my dad before he passed. For different reasons, including moving her to a closer location for medical assistance, we organised with her permission to sell her home and move her into a retirement village. With community and social functions, bus trips, and card and craft groups, she was busier and freer than she had ever been before.

'Betty next door has had some security issues,' my mum mentioned to Angus. It was a Sunday towards the end of June, and we had arrived at my mum's home so Angus could fix her curtain rod. Angus joked with her that she had been swinging from the curtain rod again, and she laughed. After he fixed the rod, he went next door to check if he could also help Betty.

That left Mum and me by ourselves. I would not know what to say when it was just the two of us. Instead, I looked at the photos on the wall. In particular, I noticed the wedding photo of my paternal grandparents. It was not a new photo, but I paid extra attention to it that day, for some reason. My grandparents looked older in the picture than I had noticed before. To fill the void of quietness, I asked my mother about it.

'Did Marsie and Grandpa marry later in life, not in their early twenties like most couples of their era?' I asked.

'Yes, in their thirties,' she replied.

Marsie looked so happy. She wore a very pretty, traditional white 1920s-style dress. It was flattering with a straight silhouette, simple lines and minimal embellishments that were true to the era. It was the type of dress that I would expect her to wear. Perhaps that's where I get my 'no-frills' attitude from.

My attention turned to Saul.

'Did they know about Saul when he was born?' I asked.

'Yes,' she said.

Without realising it, my mother had just admitted a lie that my parents maintained. When we first found out about Saul, we asked if any of our grandparents knew. They said no. My mother upheld this lie until that day.

Of course, it made me wonder even more. Was this an indication that the stories they had told us had holes? Maybe there were other secrets. Or was it just a slip of the tongue in the moment?

I wanted to know more. I turned the conversation to the fact that I wanted to write a book about finding my brother.

'How would you feel about that?' I asked.

'Dad would not have liked it if he were here, but at the same time, I am glad that we found Saul,' she said. She told me that she understood why Saul did not call her mum out of respect for his adoptive mum.

I thought of Dad saying, 'he could be in jail,' when we first discovered Saul's existence.

'Something that I have been thinking about a lot is the fact that Dad was so angry and annoyed that we went looking for Saul. Maybe he was scared. Scared of what we might find,' I said.

Mum thought about that and then said, 'You may be right.'

'How long was your engagement to Dad?' I asked.

'Fourteen months,' she replied.

I already knew that this was possibly the case, but now I heard the words from her. When Saul was born, they were engaged. Her mind must have gone back to her admission about my grandparents knowing about Saul's birth.

'It was your grandfather who said to Dad, 'Now that she's pregnant, you cannot get married till after the baby's born, and then you'll have to give the baby up for adoption.'

My paternal grandfather was such a gentle man to me that I could not imagine him saying that, but it was probably indicative of the times. From my memory, my grandfather was a tall, gently spoken man. He always seemed like a kind, heartfelt man who cared endlessly for his family. They even lived in one family home, raising their four children there.

I had previously thought that my maternal grandmother was the one who said they would have to give the baby up for adoption. It was my maternal grandparents, after all, who disowned their daughter when she fell pregnant.

I still had so many questions about those times. My thoughts then went to my dad again.

'Why did Dad not tell you about his previous marriage?' I asked, knowing that he had lied or hidden that truth from her for, I believe, three years.

'He was scared of losing me,' she said.

I was unsure if she was sticking up for him again or if he felt that way. But for whatever reason, he managed to hide this important piece of information about himself. He hid the fact that he had three daughters from his first marriage. The middle daughter passed away at an early age; the youngest, at about six months old, was placed in the care of a baby home, the same one that Saul was taken to after his birth; and the eldest of the three girls, as a three-year-old, was raised by my paternal grandmother. How did he hide that for three years?

My father was thirteen years older than my mother. When Saul was born, she would have been twenty-one and he would have been thirty-four. Even though he had a lot of age and life experience, he apparently was unable to stand up to my mother's parents. He did not insist on stopping Saul's adoption.

My father was good at telling others what to do, but conversely, he did not like anyone telling him what to do. This situation must have been an exception, because the baby did not stay with his parents. My father let them tell him what to do, or he agreed with their request.

I asked my mum that day if there were any other family secrets. She said no.

I hadn't known what to say at the beginning of our chat, but by the time Angus came back from Betty's, I found out a little more about what happened. What she did not see was me wiping away a few tears as quickly as they sprang to my eyes. Even though we had found out about Saul five years ago, it was still so raw for me.

I tried to focus on being thankful for the times that we had been able to spend with Saul. The six of us had formed great relationships. David and Saul were brothers now, and Saul had four extra sisters in his life. He was one of the six of us now.

OCTOBER 2019

It was Tuesday, the first day of my working week. Like I do every day, I looked out my window after gently opening my eyes. I could see that the sun blazed through the blinds, with the heat radiating even in the early morning—indicating a warm day, warmer than usual for October.

Luckily, I would be in air conditioning at work. But as I lay in bed, I hoped and sensed the day would be good. I trusted that I would not be saying to myself, as I did with patients at my work after we treated them for an injury, 'You would not have been expecting this when you got up this morning!'

Little did I know, as I rested for a moment longer in my bed that day, my world was about to change again in a way I could have never expected.

I was working in the treatment room, attending to patients' and doctors' needs, as I usually did. That day, I worked with my nursing friend, Reggie, with whom I had worked alongside for many years. We had a great working relationship. We understood how we both worked and shared a mutual respect as colleagues and friends.

The day continued as normal until lunchtime. I was enjoying eating my homemade salad in the lunchroom, chatting with other workmates about their day and the past weekend. After we finished talking, for some reason, I picked up my phone and checked my emails. It was not a usual thing for me to check emails during my thirty-minute break. But something told me to do so.

One of my emails caught my attention: It was from the department in Melbourne, and the subject read, 'family matters.' The email came from the Victorian-based department, now the Adoption Information Service, which had moved into the Department of Justice and Community Safety, or DJCS, earlier that year.

I was in shock, and for a moment, I fretted, an overwhelming uncertainty washing over me—would the email tell me that Saul wasn't really my brother? After my conversation with our mother a couple of weeks ago, I started to question a lot about Saul's birth. For instance, our parents had told us that the baby had been born in Melbourne. Saul was born in Geelong. I wondered about the reason for the discrepancy and whether there was more to the story.

Before I could conjecture any further, I opened the email. It was from Amanda, at DJCS. She was a different caseworker to our original caseworker, Brenda.

Amanda's email said, 'I am contacting you regarding an enquiry from a person to whom you may be related …'

'What the heck?' I said as I placed my phone down on the lunch table.

'What's up?' Asked the practice manager, also in the lunchroom.

I relayed the contents of the email to her. Her curiosity piqued.

She said, 'You have to call. Go into one of the doctor's rooms and ring her.'

My mind was in a spin. I was nervous as to what she would tell me. The suspense was getting to me, so I found a free doctor's room to make the call. My fingers trembled as I dialled the number.

Of course, Amanda did not answer her phone. My uncertainty only multiplied. What did this mean? What would she tell me? Then I slowed down my anxious thoughts and realised that she was probably on lunch herself. I would have to wait patiently until she rang me back. I replied to her email, letting her know I'd tried ringing and that I was eager to chat, and I wrote my work phone number in the details.

Reggie, just as eager to find out the news, was the person who came looking for me when Amanda called back.

Firstly, Amanda advised me that our previous case worker, Brenda, was on maternity leave. She told me that she had taken over Brenda's cases.

I felt impatient, but eventually Amanda told me, 'You have another sibling!'

My jaw dropped open. I shook my head, and I felt a bit lightheaded. Luckily, I was sitting on the edge of a treatment room bed at the time. What was going on? I barely believed what I was hearing. How could this be?

I tried to utter a word—something, anything—but no words came when I opened my mouth. Amanda, maybe sensing my apprehension, continued to tell me that we had another brother who was born in January, not quite thirteen months earlier than Saul. My mind worked overtime. I'd been worried that Saul may not have been our brother. He was, but it appeared we had another brother born before him. It meant that Saul was the second child of my parents, not the first. There was another one of us! And this new brother was the eldest of now seven siblings.

Amanda told me that our brother was born in Melbourne. Suddenly, it all made sense.

But why did our parents not tell us about another brother when we discovered Saul?

I felt relieved that Saul was still our brother. Yet, we were learning about another secret that we knew nothing about.

After we learnt about Saul, we asked our parents specifically if there was another secret, for instance, another sibling that we should know about. The answer remained no. I know that my dad preferred to keep the past in the past, but this was getting ridiculous. He had lied again. The truth never passed his lips.

Even after my father passed away, my mother still did not tell us the truth. Recently, I had asked her again if there were any other family secrets.

Saul had met Mum for lunch near his home a few weeks before, when she was on one of her community bus trips. He had asked her the same question. She had stood steadfast in her response. 'No,' remained her reply.

For the rest of the day, I felt like I was returning to those awful feelings of grief, denial and anger. How was this even possible? We had been misled by omission, not once, but twice.

I would have screamed from the rooftop if I could have climbed up there. My heartbeat was rapid; I felt like I could curl into a ball for protection. My instinct told me to run and hide; maybe then this would not be real after all. The tears welled up hard in my eyes, threatening to run down my cheeks, but they would not flow. I was in shock.

I recognised that the level of fear I felt was amplified. It was more heart-wrenching than the first time. When you get a needle or have a procedure that you have had before, you can brace yourself. But how can you brace yourself for another hit if you do not know that it is coming?

The first time, we had absolutely no indication that this would be part of our family history. The fact that our parents choose not to tell us, was one thing, but choosing not to tell us again, was a whole other level of how they failed us. They did not tell us, even when we asked, that we had another brother; it was a greater level of deception. Why did we have to hear it from a stranger, someone from the department and not our parents?

It is possible that they thought that we would not find out. The department did not find another sibling; they probably only looked for one, since none of us knew there were two. The only way that we could find out was if the other brother came looking for us. Well, that is what happened.

There were no excuses. If they had told us, we would not have discovered the truth this way. We probably would have searched for two brothers, not one. It was another choice taken from us.

This time, our eldest brother came looking for us. As we were registered with the department's central registry for adoption enquiries, our details were quick to find, making the process much easier this time. They could match our details, send me a quick email, and we would have another brother. Sounds simple now.

But the second time around, it was scarier. Way scarier.

I thought, 'This could be the brother who is in jail. Is he going to be normal? Will we get along? Could we be so lucky twice?'

We had a great relationship with our brother Saul. He was one of us. The similarities were clear. David, our younger brother, was a bit like him; they spoke and walked similarly and stood in a similar stance. We were family. Would this new brother fit in? Why did we have to go through this again? It wasn't fair. Our father had passed, so he could not answer this. But our mother could.

I was so annoyed with her. Thinking about her, I felt numb, upset and disappointed that she had lied to our faces twice now. Why did she do that? How could she do it? I did not see the purpose of lying again. I could not come up with a plausible explanation.

The relationship I have always had with my mother has never been nurturing. I had wished for more from her, and I had tried to bridge the gap in our relationship, but it didn't evolve like I would have liked.

One occasion that I tried to get closer to my mum was when I was pregnant for the third time. I thought I would involve her in the pregnancy, including coming with me to my antenatal appointments. She met me at the obstetrician's rooms for the first appointment, when I was eight-weeks pregnant. The appointment started as it normally would, with the doctor asking questions about how I was going and when I had my last period. I knew him quite well; he had been my doctor while I was pregnant with my other two children.

As per his normal practice, he performed an ultrasound in his room. I then discovered that the pregnancy was no longer viable; I had miscarried. I had no indication, not even a feeling, that during that appointment I would learn that I had miscarried.

The pregnancy was unexpected but welcomed just the same. And then, I heard the words that the pregnancy was not viable. That was an even greater shock. I did not know why this happened. I didn't know what to say or do. Instead, I sat there looking at the wall, almost like it could tell me that it wasn't true, that it was not happening. I could not escape from the truth and the sadness in my heart, aching with each heartbeat, aching for the child I would not bear. For a moment, the silence echoed around the room until it was time to leave.

'I'm so sorry,' he said, as we walked out of his room.

Out the front of the office, my mother said, 'Are you okay?'

'Yeah, maybe, it's a bit of a shock,' I replied.

Inside, I wanted to cry and express my loss, but I was unable. I think I was dazed and shocked. I certainly did not expect to learn this.

'Well, I'll be off home then,' Mum said.

I stood frozen as she walked to her car.

I decided to walk next door to my work, which was in the hospital next door. I greeted my boss. She knew that something was wrong and asked me if I was okay. I blurted out what happened. The feelings, the loss and the sadness took hold, and I cried. I needed to feel the loss of the baby that I no longer carried, and I needed to feel the sadness that my mother was unable to console me. I had sought a sense of closeness with her, but that did not happen.

Looking back, she would have been unable to console me. She had the pain of losing Nancy's twin sister when she was stillborn. What I didn't know until much later was that she had given up two of her children. That was probably why she was unable to console me. My loss may have brought back memories and pain for her. It may have been too much, so instead, she drove away. I understand that now.

There were other occasions when I tried to bring closeness to our relationship, despite memories or similarities, but I felt it was not reciprocated. She did feel for me, I am sure, but she was unable to express those feelings in my presence.

One night I watched an episode of Home and Away on TV. It was an episode where one of the characters, Dana, was sad when Irene, her friend, who was more of a mother to her than her own mother, had been diagnosed with Alzheimer's disease. Angus asked what made me so upset.

I said, 'Because I can relate and sympathise, since my relationship with my mum has not been close.'

'What do you think your mum gave you that she didn't have herself?' he asked.

I thought about it.

He went on to say, 'Sometimes, our parents try to give us what they didn't have.'

'I think a roof over our heads and stability, but I would have given all that up to have a mum,' I replied.

I remembered waking up in the middle of the night soon after we moved to Brisbane. I could hear my mum crying. She was so upset because the five of us kids did not have proper beds; we were still sleeping on our camp beds from the caravan that we'd travelled in for eight months. I am unsure if it was due to finances or time, but they were unable to get us normal beds.

The beds are symbolic of how my mother parented us. Ironically, I would have given up the normal beds to have a sense of love, protectiveness and belonging from my mum.

I guess we all see things in different ways. At that point, I still wished things were different. But if that is true—that we seek to give our children what we do not have—I sought to give my children a mum. I am grateful I could do that.

I can say categorically that our mother did love us, and she did the best that she could with what she had. I think that she was lost and unable to show emotion. I thought she had given up one son, but she gave up two. She had suffered intense trauma when she gave her sons away. To face the pain is to feel and acknowledge the pain, but she hid it from everyone, including the five children that followed, the five of us. With all that she had been through, when we needed her love or attention, she was unable to give it.

So, this new information about having another brother felt completely like a betrayal, a kick in the teeth. At that moment, I felt like my relationship with my mother was now damaged, possibly beyond repair. How could she?

Fury and resentment engulfed me at every turn. It was one thing to hide it, and another to lie about it over and over again.

It felt like a bad dream that had come back to haunt me. My parents had failed me when I was hoping for something better, now that our family was complete with six siblings. I had trusted again. How could I be so wrong and be unaware until then?

From that moment, I felt the need to protect myself. I decided not to put myself in the position of betrayal again. But really, I could not stop the betrayal; I could only stop my bad reaction. And yet, I felt my reaction was justified, since it could have been avoided.

I fully understood that my parents had done their best. I did not judge them for that. I just wanted the respect and the emotional bond that I could not have. I decided I would help my mother if she needed it. But I would put myself and my family first. That was a hard decision to make. I tried not to be judgmental in any way. But at that point, my decision was made out of pain and anger, directed at my mother.

What I could not accept was that we had been lied to again. It had been five years since we learnt about Saul. We had reacted without judgment then. Why had they chosen not to tell us this time? How dare they make that choice for us again!

I knew that I had news that would change the direction of our lives for the six of us again. It was like a sequel, another part of our journey that played out on the big screen. Part of me was in denial that this could be happening again.

But in reality, this was part of our story. I would have to share this news with my five siblings soon. How would they react? What could I say to help them when I was feeling so deflated myself?

Chapter 12

ANOTHER REVEAL

Telling one lie begets another lie that begets another lie and before you know it that lie has grandkids, great grandkids and keeps growing. It's like Lay's Potato Chips, you can't tell just one! —Sanjo Jendayi[13]

I had the unenviable task of telling my siblings. I was so overwhelmed, and I didn't know what to do. I wished that we did not have to go through this again.

I decided not to tell them over the telephone, if possible. I set about planning to get my siblings, those who lived close by, together in person. I phoned Cynthia, David and Nancy. I asked them if they could meet me early that evening at a café for a catch-up, or that's what I told them. They knew straight away that I had an ulterior motive; they just didn't know what it was.

'Why can't you tell me over the phone?' Nancy asked.

'Because I would like to see you instead,' I replied.

'What is it about?' Nancy quizzed.

'Wait and see,' I replied, cringing.

I realised that they were eager to know, and they'd be trying to guess why I wanted to meet with them. With the lies of the past, who could blame them for thinking the worst?

The four of us and our partners met at 7:00 pm that evening. On the drive there, the weather was bleak, gloomy and cold. The gloominess represented my mood well.

The others, obviously eager, had already arrived when Angus and I reached the café. I was thankful that they had chosen an outside table for us all to sit at. Since no one else was outside, it meant that we would have plenty of privacy as we chatted.

David and Nancy already started trying to guess why I wanted us to catch up, particularly on a weeknight. I do not remember what they guessed but I do remember Cynthia remained quiet.

I asked David to get Saul on the phone and Nancy to ring Jennifer. They would have known then that what I was about to tell them had something to do with our family, something big. Thankfully, Saul and Jennifer both answered their phones.

'There's another one!' I blurted out.

I heard heavy breathing and a few sighs, and then Nancy said, 'I knew it!'

Cynthia's mouth fell open, and David just stared. We were all shocked in varying degrees. Saul and Jennifer indicated their own shock over the phone.

'Saul, you're not the oldest one anymore; we have an older brother,' I said.

Then I let them know what our new case worker, Amanda, from the department, said.

I advised them that our brother's name, from his adoptive parents, was Leonard, or Lenny. He had contacted DJCS himself. As I told them, I realised it was uncanny but coincidental that he'd been given that name—my mother's brother had that name, and it was my maternal grandmother's maiden name.

I told them that he was the baby born in Melbourne and that Mum must have assumed we'd found Lenny back when we talked to them for the first time about Saul.

Lenny was raised as an only child in a Croatian-Italian family, I told them. His mother, at ninety, had the early stages of dementia. Lenny was her carer. His mother told him about his adoption a month or two before. He had lived 52 years, 8 months and 13 days—a lifetime—without the knowledge that he was adopted. His father had passed away twenty years prior, and his mother sought guidance from her church as she believed that Lenny should be aware of his heritage. She did not follow through with that for whatever reason.

Apparently, after his birth, our mum sought help for his adoption from the Gratton Street Catholic Hostel in Carlton, now the site of the Royal Women's Hospital. The hostel paperwork advised us that our dad was also part of the initial interview with the hostel. The notes stated that he'd been 'uncooperative and difficult' during the interview. Of course! That was our dad. Or did it indicate that he did not like what was happening, that he would not give the baby up for adoption without a fight?

It appeared that our mother was pregnant at nineteen, and just twenty when Lenny was born. Our father would have been thirty-three and old enough to have his say. Maybe he wanted to voice his disapproval by being difficult with the interview for Lenny's adoption. I like to think that he tried to keep Lenny. Then, when Saul was born, there was no fight left, perhaps.

Regardless, he also lived with these lies. He was uncooperative and difficult in most areas of his life; a turbulent life, to say the least. I wondered how he kept a level head at times. He hid his issues and his pain by not delving back into the past. Maybe he, like me, put things in a metaphorical room and closed and locked the door, never to think about the memories again. Possibly, this is giving him too much credit, maybe not enough. I will never know.

One thing our parents had together was the shared knowledge of the lies they kept. Most parents who went through the adoption process back then separated. But not mine.

One thing I can say with almost certainty is that if our brother Lenny had not found us, we probably would not have found him. From the information we gave FIND originally, they located Saul after looking at our birth dates. They would have started with mine and gone earlier. But once they found Saul, I assume that they did not look any further; they did not know that two brothers had been adopted out, and neither did we.

Saul, who had only just discovered that he had five siblings, was now finding out that he had another brother. He had also been lied to. That would not have been easy for him. But he was truly one of us now, lies and all.

With this new knowledge, we had another question to answer. Did we want to have contact with Lenny? Since he had searched for us, it was evident that he wanted to have contact. But did we? Did we want to bring in and learn about another sibling in our family's mess?

I asked my siblings, 'Do you want to have contact with Lenny?'

'Yes,' was the unanimous response from the five of them.

We had done it once; we could do it again, even if it would be scarier this time around.

I thought we should also talk to Mum. We needed to ask her about it, particularly why she had not told us.

'Does anyone want to go and talk to Mum about this?' I asked my siblings.

I knew that I wanted to be part of the discussion. David, Nancy, Angus, Billie, and Rose also indicated they wanted to talk to Mum.

Cynthia remained quiet; she was clearly upset, devastated and angry that she and all of us had been lied to again. She could not bring herself to face or talk to our mother. Jennifer did not even consider seeing her. She lived too far away, but more importantly, she had not had contact with our mother for years. That is another story, not for here. Saul lived too far away, also.

We agreed that we would go and see her that Sunday, after she had been to church. We told Jennifer, Saul and Cynthia that we would let them know how the chat went.

We had a plan, which was great. But I remained unsettled. I was angry and hurt, and I had hoped that those feelings would subside by the time we talked with our mum. Honestly, feelings don't just go away. I am always a firm believer in letting the thoughts and feelings sit and feel them. I did not know how long that would take. But I knew that when I was ready, I would move forward.

I wanted to hear what she had to say; that is definite. Part of me hoped that my emotions would not spill out as I listened to her words. I was overcome, consumed by the sense that it was avoidable, so unnecessary and extremely preventable. Even though I tried to feel empathy for her, she had held another secret tightly to her chest. How would that have made her feel?

But it did not need to be that way. If only our parents had been open and honest with us. Surely, we deserved that respect, that consideration.

Our father used to say, 'You make your bed, you lie in it'

Yet, he did not lie in his bed. When we found Saul, he was not regretful that he and Mum had not told us. He often said, 'The past is in the past.' He would say, 'Why delve up the past, it should be left there.'

This was another part of his life in which he had omitted the truth. Since he had passed two years earlier, he would not face us and answer our questions; only our mother would. It was unfair that she had to do it alone.

I had always wondered if there was more to those remarks from my father: 'The past is in the past.' Now, it appeared that there was. He and his wife, our parents, had kept the past in the past to themselves for many years. Now again, the past has come forward to meet us in the future. The truth could no longer be denied.

Chapter 13

HERE WE GO AGAIN

My mother said, 'Sorry, I didn't tell you.'

NOVEMBER 2019

I tried to wake myself up. My dry, irritated and puffy eyes opened ever so slowly as if the room would reveal something that I didn't want to see. The glare of the sun peeked through the blinds in my room, telling me that the day had begun—that it was real.

We were going to see my mother to have another chat. Angus looked at me and asked how I was feeling.

'I am numb and tired,' I replied. My thoughts during the night were again restless and scattered.

I felt cheated and lied to all over again. Our parents had made another big decision on our behalf. Why, for goodness' sake, why? I wanted answers.

I wondered if they thought it was better that we did not know about Lenny. Did they honestly think the truth would remain hidden? They saw how we reacted when we discovered Saul, and yet they chose to deny us the truth again.

There had been so many times when family loyalty towards my

parents was washed down the drain. And yet, we were in that position again. I found it hard at that point to feel any empathy towards our mother. Yes, she had given a child away twice, and that was huge. No one could take her pain away. But this new deception could have been avoided if only they had said to us, 'You have another brother.'

In a few short hours, we would talk to our mother. I had an overwhelming want to run and hide. Though deep down, I knew I wanted answers.

What could she possibly say that could make this okay? How could and would she attempt to make amends for the lies, to help us understand?

Today, I would have to confront my feelings by facing my mother. Thankfully, I was not going to be alone; I had my husband, my siblings and their partners. We would support each other, regardless of what we would learn.

I tried to keep myself busy until our chat by doing the household chores and our weekly grocery shop. Keeping myself busy did not stop the worries.

Before I knew it, David, Rose, Nancy, Billie, Angus and I were standing at the front door of my mother's home. She heard us knock and opened the door.

Her expression was a little bit unsure. All of a sudden, her home was full of her children and their spouses. I had no idea what was going through her mind.

We had taken a gamble that she would be home. If we had told her, she would have wondered and worried why we were coming. From experience, I am sure she would know we had come for a reason.

Our mother still lived in the retirement village. In the main living area sat her recliner chair, another lounge chair and the dining table. On the dining table was a lot of cluttered paperwork and small items scattered.

'Mum, you should probably take a seat,' I said.

'You can sit in your normal seat. I can stand. I have been sitting for hours in the car,' David said. He was still the closest one of us to our mother.

'How was camping?' Billie asked David about their camping trip. The two of them talked about camping for a moment or two.

I was getting impatient. We needed answers about Lenny, not camping. I began the conversation.

'Well, we came here for a reason. Mum, the department that found Saul contacted me again.' I paused for a moment, mostly to regain my composure. My mother then let out a noise, a sharp inward breath, a gasp, like she knew what was coming.

I had to continue, 'They have told us that there was another sibling—another brother—who is older than Saul. But like the last time, we are not here to judge you, we just want to understand.' Somehow, I managed to bring some empathy into the moment.

'Well, I do not know why we didn't use protection!' Mum said.

I gasped. It seemed a bizarre thing to say under the circumstances. Maybe she was trying to bring a little bit of humour to break the tension. I imagined that Mum wouldn't have used protection because she was Catholic, and back then contraception was considered inherently evil by the Catholic Church.

I filled her in on the information from the department, including that his adoptive parents had named him Lenny.

David stood, arms crossed and jaw clenched.

He narrowed his eyes and went straight to one of our main questions: 'We need to know if you want to have contact?'

'Well, yes, I guess it went so well with Saul, and it is a relief that this is out in the open,' she replied without hesitation.

David asked, 'What did you call him? Do you remember?'

'Christopher Mark,' she replied.

'Who knew about Lenny being born?' I asked.

'The grandparents on both sides of the family,' she said.

Then Nancy asked, 'So who wanted the adoptions to happen?'

'The family,' Mum said.

'The family ... the grandparents?' Nancy asked.

'So, you didn't go against their wishes?' David asked.

'Of course not!'

'Does Dad have any other children, apart from us and the three from his first marriage?' David then asked.

'Now is the time to come clean, to tell any truths that have not already been told,' Angus said.

'No, I don't believe so. He would be pretty honest with me, and he never told me that he had any other children.' She paused. 'So, I don't believe so.'

'Well, how can we trust that now?' David replied.

'Did Dad have a hold over you with these decisions?' Rose asked.

'No, he didn't have a hold over me. We made decisions jointly.'

'That's the hard part, you did not tell us about Saul, and now you didn't tell us about Lenny despite us asking if there was anything else we needed to know,' I said.

'I understand that. After Saul, your father and I talked about this. We had been led to believe that he had died in childhood. I don't know where we heard that, but we did,' our mother said.

Immediately, I wondered how she would know those details. The papers were closed years ago. How could they possibly know that?

I thought of Anne, the clairvoyant, whom I had seen before we found Saul. She had indicated that two sons were adopted out, but one had passed at an early age. Maybe my mother was actually remembering this.

My father and my grandparents were the only ones who knew about the adoptions. Maybe it was one of them, albeit with good intentions, who told my mother that one of the two boys had passed away in early childhood. If someone did tell her that, it's plausible that they thought it was easier for my mother to deal with her losses. At least if she did not have to wonder constantly about the whereabouts and well-being of one of her sons, it might have helped.

Anne also indicated that the eldest of the two boys had been raised as an only child and that his mother was unwell. That was correct. Anne told me that the adoptive mother somehow knew or knew of my mother, or at least our families. Now, it seemed that the clairvoyant may have been talking about Lenny's mother.

I asked, 'Do you know of any connection between his family and ours over the years?' I asked.

She told us about her father's estranged mother, our family gets weirder by the moment, who lived in Brunswick in Melbourne. She used to babysit Italian children. Maybe, just maybe, that was the connection.

The conversation shifted to the fact that no one else, not even Mum's friends, knew about the pregnancies. She told us that she was attending teachers' college at the time when Lenny was born. That pregnancy remained hidden from her friends, fellow students and teachers.

'I wore Mo-Mo dresses, they were long, tent-like dresses, made of thickish cotton that did not let light through,' she said. It seemed she could hide her pregnant belly under the dresses, and no one was the wiser.

'What size were Saul and Lenny when they were born?' I asked.

'About 4 pounds,' mother said. It seemed we were all born small.

'Did you and Dad talk about this very often?' I asked.

'Yes, we did sometimes ... only when no one else was around, I guess.'

'It must have been hard at times?'

'Yes, a bit like a mourning process,' Mum said.

'The six siblings are now going through mourning processes of their own,' Rose said.

Rose and David had had enough and decided to leave. They said bye and walked out the front door.

We had the conversation we needed to have. The sadness for us all was intense as the grieving process began yet again.

When we learnt about Saul, we had empathy and understanding, at least as much as we could without actually living through those times.

My mother told us that she was relieved to have it out in the open. We had given her the chance to move forward now that the truth was out. For over forty years, she had grieved behind closed doors. We were allowing her to open those doors, never to be closed to the truth again.

I knew that Mum had told her siblings about Saul. But she had not told them about Lenny. She had to have another conversation with them.

'Will you be alright tonight, now that we know the complete truth?' I asked her.

'I think I will have a few tears,' she said. I felt sadness for her, particularly that our father was not here to share the load.

The rest of us got up as if to leave. I turned to her, and I hugged her. It wasn't usual for me to hug my mother, but in that instant, I mustered sympathy for her, knowing that she would have to deal with this all alone.

She whispered in my ear, 'Sorry, I didn't tell you.'

I was shocked by her whisper. She had not spoken the word 'sorry' before. My sorrow and sadness for her, for all of us, intensified in that moment. I felt some closeness to her that I had never felt before.

In the coming days, I tried to comprehend what our 'new' family was. We were now a family of seven siblings, not six, or even five.

As I contemplated that, the closeness I felt for my mother was sadly short-lived. I could not get beyond her lies. I appreciated her saying sorry, but was it just a little bit too late?

I questioned my relationship with her like never before. I felt a sense of guilt and harshness as I wondered about her love, loyalty and compassion towards us and our feelings. I could feel that for her, but did she for us, for me?

A stranger had told us we had another brother. It should have been her.

I tried to muster empathy toward her. She would have suffered, and her sense of shame would have been humongous. I do not judge her for that. Nor can I comprehend what she would have gone through. She was not able to look into her babies' eyes, and she had not seen them grow into men.

But she had five other children. She saw *us* grow, but did she? Was she just a bystander in our lives, not paying attention? We suffered because of her distance and her lack of real presence. I know why now, but when I was going through that and in my earlier adulthood, I did not understand.

A fall, a scabbed knee, a lost tooth or a cut was met without help or support. When I was about ten, my inquisitive mind told me to run my finger along the edge of a piece of steel, not expecting it to be sharp. I cut my finger. No one helped me. I stood in the bathroom with water running down my bloodied finger while everyone else, including my mother, ate their dinner.

As a nurse, I now know that my finger was not given the proper medical attention it needed. In the healing process, excessive growth of granulating tissue meant the skin did not heal correctly. Instead, the new tissue grew in a domelike shape, or a raised bump, instead of being flat like normal. I used that example with my patients to let them know what can happen if their wound is not healing correctly.

Many of us have a story of sadness in our past. Many of us have had sad childhoods and sad relationships with our parents. Some are worse than others. But our situation could have been so different. We could have been told the truth and given choices in our own lives.

The days and weeks that followed were again haunted by sleeplessness and tears. My stomach would churn in knots as I lay awake thinking about every aspect, over and over again. I would analyse, interpret and evaluate each aspect, piece by piece.

I did not go to my mother and ask more questions. I do not know who I was angrier at— myself for not having the nerve or the foresight to ask the questions, or my mother for not giving me the support I needed so I could ask.

Unfortunately for my mother, my father was not able to tell us his side. She said they talked, and he told her not to tell us about Lenny. Maybe they thought they would be sparing our pain if he had passed away young.

Ultimately, those secrets held steadfast, as if they were plastered to a wall, until the wall came crashing down piece by piece.

Chapter 14

NEW ENCOUNTERS

Sometimes, the most beautiful thing is not how people meet,
but the fact that they finally found each other. —Anonymous

NOVEMBER 2019

Five years earlier, as I wrote the email to Saul introducing myself and our family, I would not have dreamt in my wildest dreams that I would be writing another email with the same purpose. But I did. This one would be addressed to my eldest brother, Lenny.

Again, I struggled to type the words on my laptop. It seemed like a jumbled mass of words. As I re-read the email, I couldn't comprehend what I had written. It was like reading hieroglyphics.

I tried to focus. Even though I used the email that I had sent to Saul as a template, I was still writing to another brother whom I had not met. How could I say it the way I wanted? What could I write that would make me feel better and give him the information he needed?

He could ask why we had not looked for him like we did with Saul. Could I tell him that we did not know about him? I felt sadness for him that we did not find him. At least his mum told him, not a stranger. But, since he did not know he was adopted, maybe it was better that we did not find him. Hypothetically, we could have torn his world to pieces had we found him.

How could I put that in his email? The answer to that would have to come later—if he asked.

I sat at my laptop until I was happy with the email. I pressed send at 8:19 pm on Tuesday, 5 November.

I have to say, as I rewrote my email here, it was a bit jumbled—like my mind at the time.

Hi Leonard,

My name is Chris. I am your sister! This is not an email I ever thought I would be writing, but on so many fronts, it is truly amazing. Thank you for looking for us. I understand that this must be overwhelming for you; it has also been for us. We have only just learnt of you in the last week. Yes, it will continue to be overwhelming for you. But we do want to make this as easy as possible. I am sending this email on behalf of all of us.

This has been awesome for us, but it must really be extremely over-whelming for you. We are very mindful of that. Of course, we understand you must have so many questions as we do about you. But we will be guided by the steps you want or the questions you want answered and to answer. We look forward to hearing from you soon with any information you may wish. We are all also on social media if you are as well. I can also give you phone numbers if you wish.

Cheers

Chris

Again I hoped that I hadn't shared too much information about us all, and I wondered how long it would take him to reply. So began a restless evening. After climbing into bed and trying to sleep, I checked my emails for the umpteenth time. Lenny replied at 10:16 pm that evening.

Hi Chris,

Glad to hear from you so quickly. Not an email I thought I'd ever be replying to, either, thinking I was an only child all my life. I've been staring at your letter for a little while now ...

Firstly, please let Mum know that I bear her no resentment whatsoever about giving me up for adoption. I think I can understand the social stigma surrounding unwed motherhood in the day. I hope she is well. I'm looking forward to getting in touch with all of you very soon. I'm not on any of the social media anymore, but my email is linked to my phone as well as my PC. On that note, my number is [...] and I also use WhatsApp. Down the track, we can do a video link perhaps, but feel free to call whenever you like, just exchange a text with me please beforehand so you don't take me by complete surprise! It still seems a little surreal to be typing this letter, but I look forward to a chat in the next day or three.

Love from your brother
Lenny

At 12:31 am, I replied to Lenny, saying, 'Thanks for your quick reply.'

To say that I could not sleep for the rest of the night was an understatement. How could I possibly go to sleep now? I sat in my bed staring at his message.

I played Solitaire on my phone—my way of getting myself sleepy enough so I could fall off to sleep. It was definitely a bad habit, but it served its purpose by allowing me to stop focusing on Lenny or Saul and to quiet my mind.

Messages went backwards and forwards from there. I mentioned to Lenny that I told our mother that he did not bear any resentment, and in return, she said she was happy for him to have her phone number. I finished by saying that I would call him tomorrow night, if he would be okay with that. I also asked him if he would like any of our phone numbers or the emails of our other siblings.

Lenny replied to my second message later in the afternoon.

Hi Chris,

Basically ... yes to all. If you hadn't already gathered, I'm also pretty keen to speak to all of you, but particularly Mum and Saul, for pretty obvious reasons, I suppose. As you probably know, today is probably more sacred to some Victorians than a Papal visit, so I'll be catching up with some mates at the local this arvo ...

Left this earlier text as is, 4 hours later I'm back ... I've just had a 3-hour chat with Saul. Feels like I've known him all my life. I'm so looking forward to talking to you and Mum, so far today is looking like a hectic one ... Stuff the local! Have more important things to do, like catching up with you. Please email any relevant contact numbers and emails you can, meanwhile, and I'll wait for your text to sort out a chat. I have unlimited calls, so not a problem to call you when you have a minute, or an hour or two. Just passed 5:00 pm now, I'll be busy for the next two hours until dinner, etc. Talk to you soon.

Cheers,

Lenny

The following morning, I checked on Cynthia and Mum by phone. Cynthia was struggling with the enormity of everything unfolding so quickly. Particularly as I could empathise with her, I was able to help her somewhat. We had our feelings and emotions to understand and work through. We had a long way to go to forgive and or heal, but we could help each other as needed.

Mum was quick to dodge her responsibilities, especially when it came to communication. She still had not told her siblings about Lenny at that stage. It was true that her relationship with her siblings, especially Aunty Lisa, had improved since my father passed. But I suggested that she ring them herself so she could let them know.

My aunt texted me that evening. 'Amazing … just wow! How exciting!'

I rang my aunty, and she said, 'It's amazing how the five of you turned out so well considering that you raised yourselves.'

By this stage, other extended family members had started learning of the news. One of my cousins, who lives in Melbourne messaged me offering her support. I appreciated the family support; it was awesome and something we needed.

My mum texted me that evening, 'Lenny and I spoke for two and a half hours tonight!'

Lenny sent us a photo of himself. I did not know what to expect. Would he be like our mum, or our dad, or one of us?

I was not ready for what I saw in the photo. He looked like Dad! It was my dad; our brother looked like him. None of the rest of us looked like him, especially not to the extent that Lenny did. The two of them had darker olive skin and dark eyes. He was skinny like my dad at the same age, and he had the same colour hair. Their facial features were similar. It was uncanny.

The next step was meeting Lenny. Jennifer met him first. At the time, her two adult children were living in Melbourne. She had already planned a trip to Melbourne to see them. Jennifer mixed her visit with meeting Lenny. They met at a pub. Lenny told me later that the wait staff assumed that they were on a first date. It would have been easy to make that assumption since they were asking questions as they tried to get to know each other as brother and sister.

Saul and David met him soon after when they flew down to Melbourne around Christmastime. A surreal moment for the three of them, I am sure, since they were three brothers meeting for the first time. They enjoyed their first of many get-togethers to come.

When I realised the significance of it being Christmastime, I thought about Anne, the clairvoyant I had been to before finding Saul. She had told me that we would find our brother before Christmas, and that would make his Christmas special. Both of our brothers were found before Christmas, Saul in October and Lenny in November, albeit it five years apart. How unbelievable is that?

Anne had told me not to give up. I felt as if we had because we hadn't found Lenny; he found us. But finally, we all found each other. Lenny chose after Christmas to come to Brisbane to meet the rest of us, but mostly Mum.

JANUARY 2020

We learnt about Lenny fewer than three months before my mother's birthday. Lenny decided to come to Brisbane so that Mum, Cynthia, Nancy, and I could meet him. He arranged to fly into Brisbane on Mum's birthday. It would make it an extra special day.

I slept well the night before despite feeling excited and nervous. I was awake and bright-eyed as soon as the sun streamed in through the window to wake me. I felt optimistic and energetic, and my mind raced with excitement. Part of me wanted to dance and be merry, and in the next moment, another part wanted to unconsciously push the feelings back down as if squashing them into a box. I did not understand these feelings; I was still on a rollercoaster of emotions.

Cynthia and I would pick Lenny up from the airport.

Trying to decide what to wear to meet my brother was a task in itself. I picked one outfit, put it on and decided it did not look right. Then I would choose another. I always put a bit of pressure on myself when choosing my clothes for an occasion. If I don't feel good in what I am wearing, I don't feel comfortable, confident or relaxed. That would show in my demeanour, by being awkward, quiet or just worried about how Lenny might perceive me. First expressions could follow me and our relationships from then on. I was definitely putting too much pressure on myself and my outfit, but I did not want to start on the wrong foot.

So carefully, I chose long-length shorts, and a dressy, flowery and happy-looking top. My brother probably would not even notice what I wore. Regardless, I was dressing for myself, so that I would feel good in the moment.

If anything, choosing my outfit carefully amplified my stress. I remember paying attention to what I wore when I first met Saul as well. But I do not remember the stress of the decision. When I met Saul, I wore a hippie-like beige skirt and a brilliant blue top that I thought would bring colour to my face. That motivation sounds funny in hindsight, but I was comfortable in that outfit. I hoped I would be just as comfortable when I met Lenny.

I was dressed and ready to go when Cynthia arrived to drive us to the airport. Along the way, we talked about how nervous we both were about meeting him. My stomach was in knots.

We arrived and parked the car in the airport car park so we could meet Lenny at the gate after his flight. When we walked into the terminal, our nerves were so great that we had to make a toilet stop straight away. I felt as if I could cry. The emotions were so strong. Somehow, I managed to keep the tears at bay.

As we walked along the escalator, I said to Cynthia, 'F**k, can you believe that this is happening?!'

The two of us were just about to meet our oldest brother for the first time, and the feelings were so intense, possibly even more so than when we met Saul for the first time.

I remembered my first meeting with Saul was filled with such intense feelings. The first hug he gave me was truly the most amazing. I can almost still feel it. How would I feel when I first saw Lenny? Would his hug be just as amazing?

Of course, Lenny's flight was landing at the furthest gate in the terminal. We giggled nervously, almost skipping the last bit. We were not going to miss out on the opportunity of seeing him walk off the plane and into our view. We could see the plane from the window at another boarding gate, as we walked past, but the door to his plane had not opened yet. The next moment, it slid open.

Quick!' I said to Cynthia, as we pushed our way through the crowd of others who waited patiently to greet those coming off the plane.

We were able to pick him out straight away. He was one of the first ten people to walk off the plane. We could see him, but he could not see us. He stood at the top of the stairs and looked around quickly. At the bottom of the stairs, he took his phone out, probably to turn it back on. Then he turned and spotted us. He walked directly towards us. He had a backpack draped over his shoulder. He wore blue jeans, and he looked very much like an Aussie bloke from Melbourne. Being from Victoria ourselves at a younger age, I could often spot another Victorian. I could tell with the few paces he walked that he had a definite swagger like that of my mum's brother—a walk that was different to the way Saul and David walked.

When Lenny got closer to us, the resemblance to our father was remarkable, albeit a younger version, giving us no doubt that he was our father's son. He was skinny and lanky with dark hair.

I looked up at him. In that moment, his eyes drew me in. I do not know why that was, except that they were intently like our fathers, a dark, dark brown.

No one spoke.

He broke the silence and said, 'I don't know who to hug first.'

And then he hugged both of us in a group hug. We were hugging our eldest brother!

When the hug finished, we all turned and started walking to the exit. We walked back along the travelator that Cynthia and I had been skipping along a few minutes earlier. I felt different as we walked with our brother; I was finally allowing myself to feel excited, not nervous or stressed.

Cynthia asked, 'How was your flight?'

'Good, a little bumpy, which was good,' Lenny said.

Lenny clarified that by saying he enjoyed flying. He told us they had some flight turbulence. Much to our surprise, he enjoys the bumpiness that comes with turbulence. Cynthia and I did not, mostly because of our lifelong affliction of motion sickness and a fear of flying. Lenny was not like that. Saul also suffered from a bit of motion sickness.

Cynthia asked, 'Do you need a coffee or just go?'

'Let's just go,' he said.

I couldn't find any words. I was a bit dumbstruck. Cynthia and Lenny did most of the talking.

'How is your mum with all of this?' Cynthia asked, referring to his adoptive mum. 'Who is looking after her while you are here?'

He told us that his cousin had agreed to stay in the family home while he stayed in Brisbane.

When we got to the car, I texted the others, 'Lenny has arrived!'

In the car, Lenny sat in the front, and I sat in the back. Lenny would be staying at my home that night. The three of us decided to go to a nice restaurant near my home for lunch. It was a gorgeous, picturesque area of my city, and I was happy to showcase some of it to my eldest brother.

Lenny told us that he wanted to have a cigarette. He, like Saul, was a smoker. So, he walked over to the edge of the marina, overlooking the boats berthed there and had a cigarette. Cynthia and I sat at a table.

I then started to feel unwell. Suddenly, I felt hot. I could feel myself sweating, and the room was spinning. I felt like I wanted to vomit. Even when feeling awful, I couldn't help but think like a nurse. I thought it might be an inner-ear infection, or my blood pressure or blood sugar levels could be low. Maybe it was just a bad case of nerves or anxiety. This had never happened before.

I was so embarrassed; how could this happen when I was meeting my brother for the first time? My body should not fail me like that. So, I sat quietly for a while, keeping the embarrassment to myself, and tried to function normally. Over the years, I had had plenty of practice at keeping things to myself. If it wasn't the emotional upheavals, it would be the moments when I had to push through migraines, somehow pretending that everything was normal. I felt that I had become adept at concealing my struggles, and this time was no exception.

When the waitress came over to take our orders, I asked for a few more moments. I could not concentrate on the menu, a bit like I had a migraine. I knew I didn't have a migraine because my eyesight wasn't affected. Whatever was happening, I had to try to focus, not an easy thing when I wanted to curl up in a ball and sleep it off.

The waitress had steered clear of our table after I asked for more time. We had to ask her to come back over. When I placed my order, I was able to focus enough.

When the food finally came out, I was disappointed. The waitress was rude and unprofessional, and it annoyed me that the restaurant did not do a better job. I was even more annoyed with myself for feeling lousy and unwell while meeting my brother for the first time. How did that even happen? I avoided telling Lenny that I felt unwell. After we ate, thankfully, the room stopped spinning. I was still sweating excessively, but I no longer felt nauseous. Each passing moment, I felt better than before, a bit more like myself again.

After lunch, Cynthia drove us to my home. As you do when you are meeting someone new, we started looking at photos. But we didn't start with pictures of us as kids or younger adults. Instead, Lenny had brought a USB stick so we could look at funny photos, not of himself, but rather humorous pictures from social media. I guess he wanted us to see his sense of humour. He also had some childhood photos of himself, not many, just a few. It was the photos of him that I wanted to see. I could see some resemblance in those photos to David, or maybe even myself.

Having Lenny in my lounge room was surreal. I could see him and hear his voice. Lenny made some hand gestures similar to ours. I discovered that he liked numbers, not like accounting but counting and numbers in general. I have an interest in numbers, and I try to tap to help me get to sleep or feel relaxed. It was too soon to notice similarities that would become apparent later, if they did at all.

An hour or so later, Cynthia drove Lenny to our mother's home so they could finally meet. Cynthia then drove herself home. I went and had a much-needed nap. I caught up on some of the sleep I had lost over the last few weeks; now that I had met Lenny, I could relax. When I woke up, I no longer felt sweaty and hot. I was refreshed and eager for the evening ahead.

The evening included dinner in a gazebo that I had reserved in another local pub. Cynthia and her family were unable to attend. David's family and mine met Lenny for the first time at the pub. My close friend, her husband and their two sons—my godsons—also joined us. I am sure it would have been a bit daunting for Lenny to meet a lot of new people, a new family to him. More so, it was the first time that he had been able to celebrate his birth mother's birthday with her—a surreal moment, I'm sure.

Lenny only found out a few months prior that he had been adopted. I am sure that he would not have suspected that he came from such a large family. He now had his biological mother, six siblings, their partners and eleven nieces and nephews. That does not include all the other relatives—aunts, uncles and cousins. It would have been a lot to take in. I realised I was a little overwhelmed just thinking about creating memories with Lenny, and I could only imagine how he was thinking and feeling.

He started making up for lost time that day. It began with him calling our mother Mum right from the start. The two of them had spoken over the phone, but that day they saw each other in person. In the gazebo at the pub, they sat together at the end of the table, and they chatted like it was just the two of them. It was uncanny, almost like they had always known each other. They forged a connection that night.

Lenny may have looked like our father, but he had a lot of our mother's mannerisms and ways. It is kind of hard to explain their similarities, but it was nice for them to be like each other. None of the other siblings looked so much like our father as Lenny did. And not one of the other siblings had such similarities with our mother as Lenny did.

When Lenny got up the next morning, I was already awake. I asked him if he wanted a cup of tea or coffee. I think he stepped into the elder brother role by telling me how to make his cup of coffee. Everyone likes their coffee their way, but this was when I noticed that my older brother was telling me what to do. Quite funny, really.

I recognised that I should have known how my brother liked his coffee, and yet I did not. There was so much about him that I didn't know. The fact that I had never woken up in the same house as my older brother before was surreal. But all these new things could become our reality. We would learn all the imperfections and idiosyncrasies about each other soon enough. It was still unfair, but our reality.

That afternoon, we drove Lenny to Cynthia's home. He would stay the night there so he could meet the rest of her family. Nancy, her husband George, and their children would also meet at Cynthia's home so they could meet Lenny. By the end of the weekend, he had met most of his immediate family.

Chapter 15

REALITY NOW

Do not dwell in the past, do not dream
of the future, concentrate the mind on
the present moment. —Buddha[14]

When Angus and I took our road trip in February 2020, aside from travelling over 5,000 kilometres, using umpteen litres of fuel and walking on countless gorgeous beaches, we also visited my two brothers, Lenny and Saul.

I had not visited them while on holiday before. We were finally able to spend time with Lenny in his hometown of Melbourne.

Unfortunately, due to time and location constraints, we were unable to visit Lenny's home. Instead, Lenny, Angus and I met our case worker, Amanda, from DJCS, for a coffee.

We arranged to meet at a café next to the departmental building where Amanda worked, right in the centre of Melbourne. I had spoken to her on the phone a few times, but it was nice to put a face to the name. I was excited to meet her and chat to Amanda about our experience with Saul and Lenny.

We met and introduced ourselves outside the café, then ordered before choosing a table and sitting down. Lenny and I had completely different coffee preferences. He ordered a strong espresso, while I ordered my usual half-strength latte.

During our chat, it was clear Amanda had a few aspects of our story that she was curious about—how we were all going, together and individually, with our new family; and how things were affecting us.

Amanda was pleased for the seven of us when we told her that things were going well. She was happy to learn that we have good contact with each other. We were all very aware that not every situation like ours had a good ending or a new beginning.

I expressed our gratitude for the support, guidance and empathy shown to us by her and Brenda, who was still on maternity leave. Their care, kindness and understanding were comforting and welcomed. Just being able to say thank you in person was amazing but truly, words could not express my gratitude. They had given so much to us by uniting us with Saul and Lenny. I will forever be thankful to them for that.

After our awesome chat, we said bye to Amanda. Then Lenny, Angus, and I walked around some shops, in and around the Bourke Street Mall. We had something to eat at Southbank overlooking the Yarra River. Luckily, like the first meal I shared with Lenny on the day we first met, I didn't feel unwell or overwhelmed.

Angus took the first photo of Lenny and me—a nice photo, I would say. We were toasting each other; Lenny had a beer, and I had an apple cider. I don't like my picture being taken, but that one wasn't too bad; it captured the moment well.

Then Lenny decided to take us to a bar, with a difference, around the corner. To get to it, we had to walk through a narrow doorway and up about ten or twelve steep steps. I felt a bit apprehensive even walking through the doorway. I wondered where he was taking us, but I was trusting my elder brother.

At the top of the stairs and through the doorway, I was pleasantly surprised. It was a quaint bar. The walls were lined with books of all types, shapes and colours. The differences didn't stop there. When we approached the bar itself, we could see that it had the most exotic alcoholic drinks. We all settled in and had a couple each.

It was good to spend time with Lenny alone, just Angus and me. The time was short, but we enjoyed each moment. I had been able to spend time with my brother, something of a rarity for obvious reasons.

That evening, to go home, he took the train. The ride home took him a lot longer than it should have due to rail line issues. We all had problems getting home that night. We could have spent more time together in the city, and maybe the problems we faced wouldn't have happened. But that was not meant to be.

The issue for Angus and me began when we decided to tick something off our bucket lists. Both of us had always wanted to ride in a pedicab. Angus and I were walking back to our accommodation, and we saw a few pedicabs for hire. So, in the spur of the moment, we decided to get a ride back to our room, not realising that it would go so horribly wrong so quickly.

The rider of the pedicab was on a working holiday from overseas. He did not know the Melbourne roads well. He peddled so fast as he navigated with his phone at the same time; not a safe thing to do at any time, let alone at night and in unfamiliar territory.

He accidentally peddled up the wrong ramp into oncoming traffic.

All I saw were the headlights of the traffic heading straight for us. I was petrified. In that moment, I had visions of us not even making it to our accommodation. I wanted to get out of the pedicab. Instinctively, I reached to open the door to get out. I felt like it would be safer if I walked. Silly. Angus grabbed my hand and convinced me to stay inside.

Luckily, out of nowhere, there was a break in the traffic. We did not see any other headlights coming towards us, giving the rider enough time to pedal safely to the top of the ramp. We returned to our accommodation unscathed and in one piece.

I paid the rider a tip for getting us to our destination safely, and because he must have been just as scared as we were. It could have been much, much worse. I hope that the tip allowed him to finish early.

After the rest of our holiday, we returned home, just before the first COVID-19 lockdown. Contact with Lenny was more sporadic and by telephone only. I tried contacting him as often as I could during the lockdowns, especially as he lived in Melbourne. During the pandemic, times were tough. Lenny had to stay home as his mother's caregiver. He was careful to avoid contaminating their home with COVID.

Angus and I were essential workers. For myself, even though I was an essential worker, I had to take a second job because of my diminished capacity; I could not go into the homes of my elderly patients for their home visits, due to the regulations at the time. Some of my patients would have benefited and wanted outside contact, especially if they lived alone, and they usually enjoyed a lot of social contact. It was different when driving to work during those times. The roads were quiet, with limited road traffic.

During this time, partly due to what was happening around us all, and partly the result of working two jobs, I became quite unwell. I had a throat infection. I had to be hospitalised a couple of times due to a secondary infection in my lungs and heart. I often wonder how someone healthy can all of a sudden have a heart issue—pericarditis, which is inflammation of the pericardium, or the tissue surrounding the heart, causing sharp chest pain and other symptoms.

The next time we saw Lenny was for David's 50th birthday in

December 2023. Lenny flew to Brisbane for the party. He then caught two trains to Helensvale and was picked up by family there.

The celebrations began on Friday and continued throughout the weekend. It was another family camping trip to celebrate a birthday, held at a caravan park on the Gold Coast. Around thirty to forty family and friends celebrated with David and his family. Most of us stayed in caravans or cabins at the caravan park. Lenny stayed in a cabin. As he had an extra room, our mother shared the accommodation with him. Saul and Tillie also stayed in a cabin, a couple of doors away.

One of the highlights was the Saturday night dinner. We invaded the camp kitchen, all of us bringing a plate to share and our drinks. My mother has always been a wine drinker. In the past, when she drank wine, she would try to get us in a bear hug; she would squeeze so tight that it was hard to get out of it at the time.

It started like any other celebration with speeches. As the speeches were concluding, my mum decided to say something. Maybe she did not realise that she said it aloud, or maybe it was something she had wanted to say. I did not ask her why she said what she said. I may one day, but so far, I have not.

'Well, you were the only one planned!' she said to David.

Cynthia, Nancy, our daughters and I were all standing together near our mother. We were close enough to hear what she said, every word. Our mouths dropped open.

Why did she say that, so we could all hear?

All I could think was, why would you not continue by saying, 'But I loved our family, all of our children.' She did not say that then or at any other time after.

Even if a pregnancy is not planned, there's an opportunity to embrace the joy and gratitude that comes with expecting a child.

Regardless of the circumstances, the joy of a new pregnancy and then the birth of your child is a beautiful experience like no other.

My mother, though, had to give up the first two of her children. That is an experience that I would imagine to be unbearable. How you move beyond that, I do not know. My parents did manage to move on somehow. They had more children, giving them the profound and beautiful experiences they had missed with the two eldest boys.

It is not for me to say that they should have embraced all of their children, but when the comment includes you, it involves your emotions—and they should have embraced us all. When you say that you only planned one of six pregnancies, and your family hears those words, that is inexcusable.

As a mother myself, I struggled with that notion. I think differently, and as such, my kids have always been the light in my life. I have always been thankful for them, and I would not change a single thing about them. They are my children, and they are amazing. I tried my darndest to give them the mum that I wanted. I think I have done that. Most likely, there will be other things they will not like about me. I hope, though, that those things are not lifelong or unsettling in any way.

But when I heard those six words spoken, the timing of that and other things wasn't so good for me. Finances, as for many others, were challenging. Not only was there the anguish of the pandemic, but I had health issues, and I neared the point of burning out.

I quit my job. I had worked there for seventeen years, and I knew the time had come to move on. But financially, it may not have been the best move. I also struggled with a lack of self-esteem, and my mother's comment affected me deeply. I allowed my monkey mind to get the better of me, and I felt that I had plunged into deep sadness and despair. I don't think it was a depressive state; I was more likely despondent. But I did not feel like there was a way out of feeling so down. I always try to be positive and see the best in everyone and everything. I found accepting that hard.

It did not help that Christmas would be different that year from every other year. My daughter was on an overseas holiday with her partner and his family. That was good for her; she had only previously ventured overseas with the seven of us to New Zealand. Whilst happy for her to venture overseas, I still missed her. Our other children also had other parents or the parents of their partners to see, and so we did not see as much of them as we would have liked. After we did see them, Angus and I hooked up our caravan and drove to NSW to stay with my siblings in a caravan park managed by Nancy and George.

I cried that Christmas morning. The only other time I cried on Christmas morning was when I bought my parents drinking glasses. When they opened them, I felt bad that I hadn't given them a nicer, more personalised gift.

We arrived at the caravan park around 3:00 pm. David, Cynthia, their families, and one of our cousins and his partner were also camping. It was nice to catch up with them all and wish them a Merry Christmas. Then on Boxing Day night, we all sat around the campfire flickering under the night sky. The conversation around the fire was also good, or so I thought.

As we wouldn't be together for the New Year's celebrations, I initiated a discussion by suggesting that each person around the fire reflect on the positive and the negative aspects of their past year. I also invited them to share their aspirations for the coming year and what they wanted to carry forward from this year to the next. One by one, we all talked. Mostly, they all spoke with hope for the year to come.

When I spoke, I told them that the positive aspect of my year was being grateful and fortunate to have narrowly avoided burnout. I also expressed the negative aspect of my reduced work hours, which led to financial stress. I wanted to highlight this because my priorities had changed, and I'd begun to reflect deeply on myself and my direction.

I went on to say that I was greatly affected by my mother's comment about David being the only planned child. Part of my self-reflection involved a deep desire to let it go, forgive my mother for what she said, forgive myself, and move forward into the new year.

When I started talking, I didn't plan to talk about this. At that moment, I told them I had struggled with her words. I wanted them to know that I was there for them also, if they felt the same way.

'I think you have taken it out of context,' David said.

Nancy and I both jumped to defence. We strongly voiced that she could have added to her comment by saying how much she loved having all of us, that we were the best part of her life, or anything positive to support the situation, but she didn't.

In the diminishing light, no one was able to see the tears in my eyes. I sat quietly, not saying another word, and after the last person spoke, I said goodnight and went to bed. I cried in my bed silently that night.

The next morning, sitting outside our van, I chatted with Cynthia, who was reassuring and supportive.

Then I talked with Nancy, who said, 'I have always known that I was a mistake.' I sometimes joked about it—Mum wanted a boy after three girls—and then Nancy came. I never meant a word of it; she knew I was only ever joking.

I don't recall Mum telling Nancy years earlier that she had been a mistake. I knew my mum could be cruel, but I also knew that Nancy had lived with that notion since then. She told me she had dealt with it over the years, and she was okay with it. I still felt sadness for her knowing it for so long, and for us all knowing it then.

Even though our parents had not planned for us, we are here, alive and living life. The planning may not have been there, but we're here for a reason. We are learning, loving and making the most of life. I knew that I had to get over what she had said, but that was only part of the problem.

Towards the end of my conversation with Nancy, David joined us. After a few minutes of general chit-chat, he said he was going back to his caravan for some shade, as the sun had risen higher and beamed down on us. I thought he might have asked if I was okay, but he did not.

I think that David did not want to see our parents in a bad light. Everyone has their interpretation, and he is certainly entitled to that. Unlike him, I was not ready to give my mother the benefit of the doubt, that I had misinterpreted or that she did not mean what she said. As my father would say, 'There's a lot of truth in gest.' Overall, David was not one of the ones who hadn't been planned. He couldn't really understand how I felt.

Angus and I had breakfast. We then started to pack up our campsite and said bye to everyone before heading home. We arrived home almost three hours later. I was happy to be home and sleep in our bed that night. I knew this was my time to concentrate on the present and allow myself to move forward. I did not want to dwell any longer.

We saw Lenny next when he came to Queensland for a camping trip with David, Saul and Tillie at Stradbroke Island. Angus and I caught the water taxi over and met them on the island. We spent a fun-filled day with them all; I laughed so hard that day that my cheeks were sore. It was a great day spent with my three brothers, Tillie and Angus.

Lenny also came to Queensland when our mother was unwell and in hospital. A few days before his arrival, we were advised by the emergency doctor to talk to her about her end-of-life. Definitely, not the easiest conversation to have with your mum, but Cynthia, David and I talked with her about her wishes.

When Lenny came, he didn't know what to talk to Mum about. Does anyone know what to say when they may not see that person again? I reminded him about how he and Mum talked non-stop when they first met—when he came for her birthday in 2020. He had known her for just over five years. He was lucky in that sense; he did not get to meet our father.

When I took him to see her in the hospital, his uncertainty was short-lived, and they talked well together. It was undoubtedly nerves when he said he did not know what to say. It was good for her to see him, and him to see her. That same weekend, Mum's two sisters came up from Victoria to see her. It was also good for them to be together.

That was a few months ago, and our mother is still here. She has gone back to her normal life, well, her new normal life. She has been given a new lease on life, and the rest is up to her. We give her the support she needs, and that's okay. I have previously written that I would not go out of my way for her, but that was a bit short-lived. Despite everything, she is our mother.

My mum and dad.

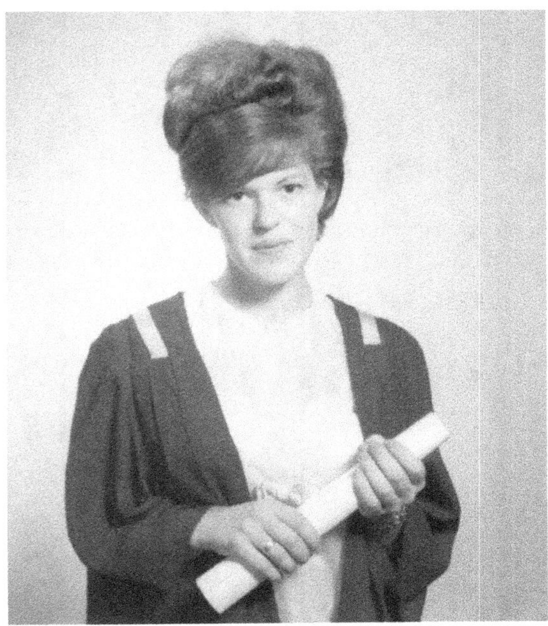

My mum.

Above: (L to R) Mum, my great grandmother, me being held by my grandmother, and my sisters, Jennifer and Cynthia in the pram.

Below: (L to R) Me, Saul and Lenny.

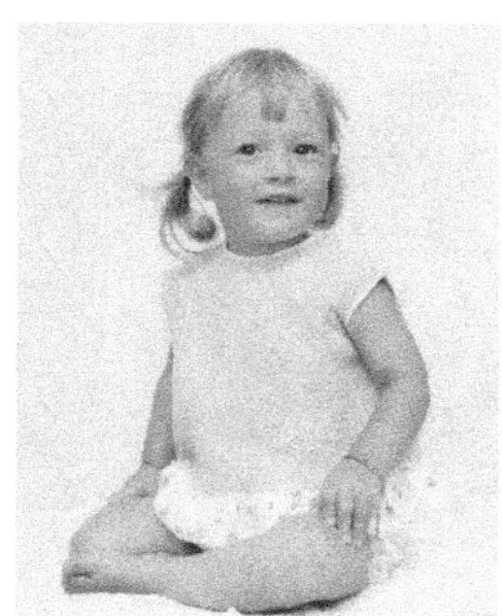

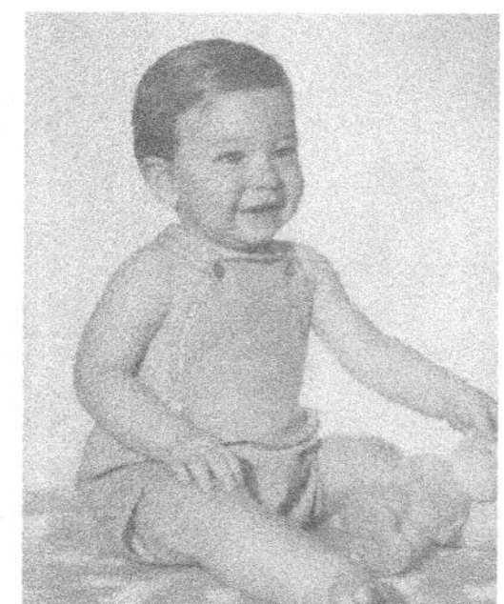

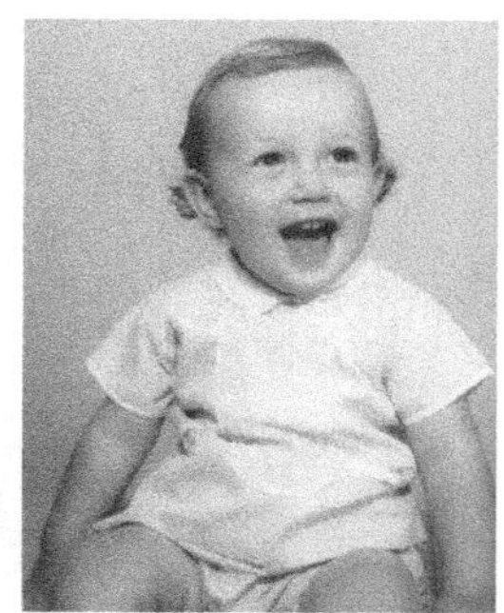

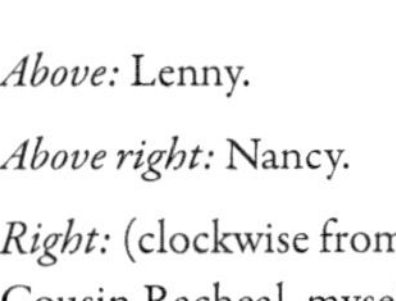

Above: Lenny.

Above right: Nancy.

Right: (clockwise from back) Jennifer, Cousin Racheal, myself, Cynthia, Cousin Jason, David and Nancy.

Below: (clockwise from back) Me, Jennifer, Cynthia, David and Nancy.

Lenny

Saul

Me

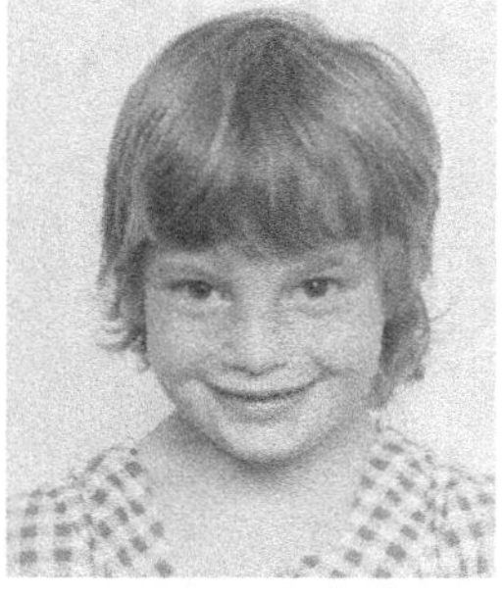

Jennifer

Cynthia

David

Nancy

PART THREE

MORE FAMILY TIES

Chapter 16

WHEN WILL THE SECRETS END?

Sand keeps secrets better than mud. —Delia Owens[15]

I looked over at my clock; it said 3:21 am—another hour had ticked by. If I closed my eyes, my monkey mind kicked in. It was as if I were watching another movie, scene by scene, in my mind. I would call that movie *When Will the Secrets End?* From experience, I knew that the only way to stop and quiet my mind was to write. I decided to get up and go into my study and type what was on my mind on my laptop. This is what I wrote.

My father had another family, three daughters from his first marriage: Lee, Elizabeth and Julie. I had always known this. However, there is more to that part of the story, which makes up part of this story.

I was close to Lee, the oldest of the three girls. She was raised mostly by our grandmother, Marsie, one of our aunts and Dad at intervals. Lee and I didn't see each other as half-sisters, but sisters. I pretty much grew up with her whenever we visited my dad's family. I would stay with Marsie and Lee. Some of my siblings would also stay in their home, but the others would stay with my parents in the home of my dad's twin brother.

When staying at Marsie's home, I would sleep in Lee's room. We would spend a lot of amazing times, especially when we were supposed to be asleep, just talking. It was the everyday things that we shared mutually that are special moments to me today—our conversations, the times we walked around the shops, going to the beach or even just sunbaking in the backyard. I remember her son walking behind the two of us as we walked around the shops. He'd call after her, saying, 'Mrs Wobblebum!' We would all laugh.

At fifteen, I had the honour and pleasure of being Lee's bridesmaid for her second wedding. I spent hours on a bus travelling with my father from Brisbane to Geelong so that I could be part of her wedding. Again, I stayed at Marsie's home. Lee was still living there before her wedding. Dad stayed with his brother.

During that visit, Lee and her music producer husband-to-be, Gerry, took me to a John Farnham concert. I was a fan of Johnny, as he was known then, and I hoped that we might meet him afterwards, as Gerry was promoting the event. But even more so, I was excited to be attending my first concert with my sister.

Before going to the concert, I had my first ever drink, Midori and lemonade. It tasted amazing. I felt so grown-up having a drink with my sister. The Midori tasted so sweet and luscious, making it easy to mistake for a non-alcoholic drink. Though I would not have known the difference then.

When we arrived at the concert, the thrill of being there would have been evident in my wide-eyed smile. I felt so privileged and fortunate to watch from the upstairs balcony. Lee and I danced and sang. I was not such a good dancer, nor a good singer. Not that anyone could see my dance moves, nor could anyone hear my singing voice.

All of a sudden, I felt hot, nauseous, dizzy, and my sight narrowed. My legs must have given way, and I woke up on the floor a moment later, feeling dizzy with the room spinning. Someone carried me outside to get some fresh air. As soon as the fresh air hit my face, I felt like I was going to pass out again.

It must have been the effects of the Midori, the heat, the joy and excitement that I was experiencing. Whatever the reason, the night ended abruptly, compared to what I had expected. After sleeping it off, I felt okay. I still like the taste, but I have only had the odd drink of Midori since then. Unfortunately, due to that incident, I didn't get to meet John Farnham. I was so disappointed.

Lee had the most amazing, beautiful singing voice—a voice of an angel, I thought. I loved listening to her sing. Gerry had a recording studio, and I felt privileged and honoured to be there when she recorded a song, 'You've Got a Friend', in Gerry's studio. I will never forget the joyful smile that spread across her face as she looked at me while singing each word. I think she was as excited about my being there as I was.

Lee and I shared many happy memories, many secrets, and many moments meant for sisters. I am forever grateful for those times and for the bond that I shared with her.

When she passed away by taking her own life at the age of forty-five, the devastation for me was insurmountable. I have always wondered why. For many years, I felt she did not mean to do it; it was merely a call for help. That may have been my way to cope with what happened. Either way, I still feel it, often with tears, when I think or talk about her today, over twenty years later. From my experience, when a family member takes their own life, the pain never leaves. But you learn to forgive and accept.

When someone takes their own life, there is a coroner's inquest, which delayed her funeral. When they released her body, her mother organised the funeral. My parents, Jennifer, Nancy and I went to the funeral. Jennifer and I arranged to meet at the Melbourne airport; she organised a car and we travelled together from there.

While sitting on the plane, I decided to write about Lee. I wish I still had those words today, but unfortunately, they were lost in the many moves I have had over the years. I aimed to say this at her funeral as part of the eulogy. I wanted to talk about who she was, not what she did.

When Jennifer and I chatted on the way to the funeral, it was clear we were both in a state of denial. For ourselves, we decided we wanted and needed to see that it was true; that she was truly gone. We called the funeral home and asked if we could view Lee before the service. They had to delay the ceremony due to our request, but we were not concerned about that. We got the answer we needed, but not the answer we wanted.

During the service, I remember a little sparrow flying around in the courtyard beside the chapel. I was lost in the sparrow merrily flying around with no worries, no fuss, and no other birds threatening her survival. It reminded me that Lee was free, that she had no more pain. I also gave my eulogy, another comforting thing to do on the day, for her and me.

It took me many years to forgive myself for not knowing there was something wrong. To this day, I still believe that she did not mean to do it. As my way of coping with her loss, my guilt, and my grief, I need to believe that she did not intend to succeed. It was just a cry for help that took a drastic, heartbreaking, and tragic turn. She was my dear older sister, and I could not believe that would be the end.

Today, when I think of her or talk of her, my eyes well up with tears. It's hard, so hard, to let go when something like this happens. As I said, you learn to accept, but you never forget.

I was unable to share a bond with my other two sisters from my father's first marriage, due to timing and dynamics within the family. The second daughter, known as Elizabeth—her birth name was Kristine Elizabeth—died at fifteen months, another tragic and heartbreaking passing. She passed away before I was born.

Interestingly, my father named me after her. We shared the same first and middle names with different spellings. And, of course, the same last name. Even though we never met, knowing we had identical birth names gave me a surprising sense of connection to her.

After the passing of Elizabeth and due to a complete marriage breakdown, my father's first wife left, leaving him with two daughters. Lee was three years old, and Julie, the youngest, was less than six months old. Marsie, already an older lady, took in Lee since my dad was unable to care for her.

They placed Julie into care at a baby home, since she was still a baby and Marsie was unable to care for her and an active three-year-old. My father paid for her care. I do not know how long she remained there. For the most formative years of her life as a baby and toddler, she didn't have someone in her family to feed, house or clothe her. Nor did she have a parent to hug her, especially when she needed consoling, love and care. And yet, her family continued to live their own lives outside of the home where she lived. I cannot imagine that. I feel deeply sad and angry that my family did that to her. The marriage breakdown of her parents should not have led to her paying the ultimate price.

One of the workers from the facility took a liking to Julie. She would take Julie home to her parents' house for the weekend. The parents later adopted her. What I fail to understand is that her adoption had not been finalised until she was seven. How long had she remained in care? How long did she go to her adoptive parents' home on the weekends before she went there permanently? Why was another child, a daughter, adopted out when it could have been avoided?

I understand to some extent why they put her into care, but I fail to understand why they agreed for her to be adopted. I empathise with the fact that Marsie was unable to care for both sisters, especially when Julie was so young. But why didn't they take her back into the fold of the family after the baby stage? She would have been seven when my father signed the adoption papers. Why did he believe it was better for her to be adopted rather than come back into the family? Or did he even think that way? I will never know the answers.

The sad part is that she would have known her adoptive family better than her own relatives. I understand that Julie did not have an easy time as an adopted child. How was that fair? It brings me such sadness. Who would not have a tough time after being abandoned by their family? I hope that she was not aware of those adoption details, but I think she was.

Sadly, I did not grow up with Julie as I did with Lee. The last time I remember seeing Julie, I would have been seven years old, and she would have been about eighteen. She came to our home to talk with my parents and Lee. The five of us kids were told to play outside while the adults talked. From what I remember, an argument may have broken out between all or some of the adults. Whatever the reasoning, Julie left our home, and we did not see her again. I do not blame her for that. I hope that she found some peace with it all, but I have my doubts. That saddens me also.

She also passed away in her early forties.

I had dream a few years ago that there was another girl in our family. In the dream, this person contacted us. I remember that she was just like us. That made me feel good in the dream. I believe that dream came true.

My sister Julie had three children. Because we had been estranged most of my life, I did not meet any of her children. Then, in December 2023, Julie's daughter, Addison, made contact. She inadvertently contacted my brother David, and understandably, she had a lot of questions about the family. David gave her my contact details, thinking that I would know more of the answers to the questions. Cynthia and I talked to Addison over the telephone soon after.

She sounded so much like us. But Addison had struggled with the passing of her mum when she was young. I could understand that. I hoped that we could help her and be there for her as her aunts whenever she needed.

I got to know Addison. I think we bonded with similar ideals and interests. She is a mum, a wife and a local business owner. It was so nice to hear that she was doing well and to get to know her a bit over the phone. We live about 1,200 kilometres from each other.

During our phone conversations, it was clear we both felt the same way as we each discovered details about our family or Julie that the other did not know. I realised there were more lies or untruths I still did not know. That was hard.

I wish I had looked for and found my sister Julie in my early adulthood so that I could have known her. To hug her and laugh with her, to do everyday things with her. For the lost time and the lost memories that we did not create together, I feel a deep sorrow in my heart. But mostly for not knowing and seeing my sister for who she was. I will never get that chance back with Julie.

Thankfully, I have a chance to get to know Addison. For that, I am grateful. We have spoken on the phone many times. I hope that we are building a family bond, and I am optimistic that we will meet in person someday soon. Hopefully, then I can hug her, laugh with her and create memories with her. Until then, messaging and telephone conversations will do.

While Angus and I were on our holiday to the Great Ocean Road in February 2020, we visited the graves of my three sisters. It is a strange thing to do when you are on holiday, but I had not visited Julie's or Elizabeth's graves before. It just happened that we were driving near Julie's hometown, and I looked up the address of the local cemetery. We were only about eight kilometres away. We changed our destination on the GPS and drove directly there. I did not know where she was buried, but luckily, the names of those buried there were listed on the walls of a shed-like structure near the entrance of the cemetery.

From there, I found her plot easily. Her headstone read: 'Dearly loved mother …' I knew from Addison that she was loved, but seeing those words really helped me feel some peace and calmness for her and for me. I was grateful to feel a sense of connection to her in that moment and extremely thankful to see her final resting place.

All three of my sisters were buried in different cemeteries. I visited Elizabeth's grave on a weekday, allowing me to go into the cemetery office to find out where she was buried. The cemetery staff directed me to her grave. I found her grave to be the saddest of them all, mostly as her plot does not have a headstone, unlike all the others in her section of the cemetery. It saddens me to think that she may have been forgotten. Her sisters passed over twenty years ago, and both of her parents passed away within the last ten years or so. I was the first person in the family to visit her grave in many years, I believe. One day, I will put a headstone on her grave, then she can finally be at peace.

While standing at Elizabeth's grave, Angus could sense my sadness. He said to me, 'Why don't you write a note to her?' I thought that was a great idea. I wanted her to know that someone cared. So, we walked back to our car to find some paper and a pen. While I was writing the letter, a car accident occurred about 100 metres down the road. We might have been driving and been involved in that accident had I not been writing that letter.

I walked back to her grave and placed the letter in a flower holder on her grave. I did not write the name she was known as, Elizabeth, but rather her birth name. I wrote to Kristine from Christine. It would have been bizarre if someone came across that letter on another day.

Dear Kristine,

I am so sorry that you passed away at such a young age. Please know that I think about you often. Love you, Christine xx

My father and his first wife had eloped. About eight months before their wedding day, his wife had a son. His name is Gregory. He was also adopted out. Gregory may be my father's child, his first child.

Several years ago, Gregory's partner placed an advertisement in the local paper. The ad was in the 'Desperately Seeking' section. I have removed the identifying information.

Looking for mum ... SEEKING information on ..., who was born in ... about ... 1938. Married to ... on February 10, 1956, in Geelong. She was my partner's birth mother. His birth name was ... and he was born ... in 1955.

My uncle saw the advertisement and telephoned my father.

'No, he's not mine; he's my first wife's. I will ring her and let her know,' my father told my uncle.

More lies. How would he have her phone number after all these years?

He told us a different story, that he contacted them by ringing the phone number in their ad. I do not know how the conversation went except that he told them to never contact him again. Could we even trust anything that our father said, after all the lies he had told us? If he did, I feel awful for Gregory. He was rejected twice, which is simply not good enough.

If Gregory is my half-brother, I feel bad that my father may have treated him that way. He did not deserve that. I hope that one day I will have the opportunity to meet him and determine if he is our half-brother. I believe that if he is my father's son, he is a brother to me, just like my other three brothers. A couple of years ago, I had a dream where my father told me that he had another son. Was that Gregory or someone else altogether?

The legacy my father left is his children. He didn't leave much in the way of property or money. He only had himself. I hope that we all leave a legacy from our lives; something that's meaningful and long-lasting. A person can leave a meaningful legacy through their children, even if they weren't good parents.

My father fathered a lot of children. He had three or four children with his first wife and eight from his second marriage. That's a lot of children. From them, he had grandchildren and great-grandchildren. Unfortunately for him, he did not have a bond with most of his children. As his children, we have not followed in his footsteps—we have amazing, mutual bonds with our children and our extended family. I guess his legacy taught us not to be that person. I am grateful that I am not.

Chapter 17

TO FORGIVE OR NOT?

*Mistakes are always forgivable, if one has the
courage to admit them.* —Bruce Lee[15]

*When you forgive, you heal. When you
let go, you grow* —Anonymous

I never thought I would write this book. It has been the cathartic
process that I needed to support and verify what happened, from my
point of view as the sister affected by the adoptions of my two brothers.
When they say it takes a village to raise a child, the same can be said
when a family is affected with hardship, shame and trauma. It affects
the village or the whole family for generations to come. I am just one
part of that whole family.

To say that this affected me is an understatement. I am not down-
grading what my parents went through, but this also affected the course
of my life. This chapter is the pinnacle of my journey. A journey that
has culminated in whether or not I forgive and heal.

I discovered that I do need to find forgiveness for all those
involved—my parents, both sets of grandparents, maybe even my
aunt—for how they wronged me and all of my siblings.

The question remained, 'Could I forgive them?'

Before I delve into that, let's consider what the concept of forgiveness is. Why is it so important for us to find forgiveness?

Forgiveness is good for our body and our soul. It does not mean that we let the other party off; we are simply allowing ourselves to let go of anger, resentment, and negativity. Effectively, we are stopping the blame game that keeps us trapped in the cycle of suffering until we decide to act, to seek peace, joy and compassion and move forward.

Dr Fred Luskin, a leading expert in forgiveness for over twenty years, said: 'Forgiveness is the powerful assertion that bad things will not ruin your today even though they may have spoiled your past.'[17]

On an emotional level, as we forgive, we can heal. It can be a roller-coaster of a journey, but through healing, we can transform our pain into strength, empowering us to move forward and live life.

I love the quote in the epigraph above, 'When you forgive, you heal. When you let go, you grow.' It brings a feeling of excitement and a deep sense of relief; when and if I can forgive, I can grow and move forward within my own life. By allowing myself to let go, I am saying that those things no longer control me. The pain will no longer cause me heartache and anguish. Effectively, it would mean that enough is enough. But can I do it?

Forgiveness can massively affect your physical health. Stress and the inability to regulate your emotions and reactions that come with being unable to find forgiveness could cause physical stress to your body. In moments like these, I feel that my mind is blocking my ability to seek forgiveness. Do I want to re-awaken what I have buried so deeply? Am I ready for that?

I still feel the sharp pang of profound sadness and despair. It may all be too much. Can I learn to live with the feelings, to investigate them, or will I choose to hide from them as I have done in the past?

Do I really want to be free of the pain, anger and bitterness that I have stored deep inside me? To do that, I will have to face facts, and be reminded and probably relive what has happened. Can I bring myself to let go and look towards my future without being weighed down? I knew that if I wanted to feel the joy without feeling this burden, I would have to let it go. I also knew, it wasn't going to be easy.

When I started writing this chapter, I became overwhelmed by brain fog and noticed myself becoming less alert. I was unable to concentrate. I could see the ripple in my eyes and the sudden pain in my forehead—the beginnings of a migraine. So, I stopped writing.

It took me a week to come back. I procrastinated because of the pain it caused me as I examined my feelings as I wrote. There were no tears, but I feel that I was delving back into the extremely deep pain.

Another facet was the guilt that weighed heavily on me, and I found it hard to let that niggling feeling go. There's something deeply intense about putting my life on the page, as well as the lives of my family. Did I have the right to do that? Should I? I knew my dad would not have been supportive. I have been passed down the notion that certain things should be kept behind closed doors, the way my father wanted. But what does that achieve? Nothing, especially not forgiveness or healing.

What motivated me to continue writing was the hope that my journey would help others. We are all human, we all make mistakes, and we could all learn from them. My father thought I should learn from his mistakes, but when you do not experience mistakes for yourself, how can you possibly learn? Additionally, we can heal for ourselves, our families, our ancestors—past, present and future.

I will never forget, but maybe, in some respects, I can forgive.

Forgiveness is not for those I would be forgiving; it is for me. I would be replacing the negative feelings towards them with a sense of goodwill or, at the very least, acceptance of them and their wrongdoings.

The first quote at the beginning of this chapter, '*Mistakes are always forgivable, if one has the courage to admit them,*' really resonated with me in this moment. I am not one to let my mistakes define me. I will stand up and say sorry, but can others say sorry to me?

Indeed, my dad did not admit his mistakes. Quite possibly, he did not dare to admit to his errors of judgment. But I do not live by his faults. I am not perfect, that is also true. But I can do what I need to do for myself, in the moment.

Moving on is not an easy road. It will not happen just because I want it to happen; it will take effort and time on my part. I hope that if you relate to my situation, you also find solace, forgiveness and healing as you let go and grow.

With a heavy heart and a feeling of dread, let's move on.

For clarity's sake, I will tackle this process of forgiveness by addressing each of my family members this relates to, starting with my father.

DAD

My father was the main person who had wronged me over the years, and there is more that I need to forgive him for than any other person. He has wronged me, my sisters, my mother, even though she will not admit it, and almost any other female with whom he has had contact.

A father is someone who is meant to love and care for you, look out for you and do right by you. He should see you, be present, supportive and guiding as he helps you be the best version of yourself. My father did not teach me by example. He had many words of ethical and emotional wisdom, but he did not live according to those words himself. Maybe he was unable to live true to his own words. It may have been that he wanted us to do the things he couldn't do himself.

Although my mum tried to give us what she did not have, I don't know what my dad did not have that he tried to give to us. Maybe he wanted us to do better or to be better.

What I do know is that he did not have to attend boarding school like my mother. He was part of his family. He was mischievous, that is true. It is possible that my dad bore the brunt of the punishment for those mischievous acts. But I do not think that would contribute to the person he was.

His first family collapsed after Elizabeth passed away, and his marriage broke down. It is quite possible that what he went through then shaped who he became when he became our father.

Regardless, he showed me how not to be as a person, a parent or a family member. He used to say, 'Learn from my mistakes.' I would always scoff at that. Everyone makes mistakes; mistakes are our biggest life lessons. The life lessons I received from him were how not to be, rather than how to be. That is how I would learn from his mistakes.

My father did things he shouldn't have done. He often behaved like a tyrant, an abuser. He was chauvinistic and often someone you would not cross or approach when he was angry. I am sure he had a lot of demons gnawing at him. With all that he had been through, it isn't surprising.

In his way, he did love us. I can see that now, but during those years, I could not.

It wasn't always bad. If I asked him about something, he would be present and tell me almost everything he knew about the subject. We travelled around south-east Australia in a caravan for nine months in the mid-1980s, when travel like that was not as common or popular as it is today. One of the life lessons my father and my mother taught me was to spend time with our extended family. In our immediate household, apart from being family, my siblings and I, and our children, also chose to be great friends.

Now the question is, can I forgive him for the things he did to me both as a child and then as an adult when we discovered that we had brothers?

To answer this question, I want to go back a couple of years, when I was participating in a retreat run by two of my close friends. During the retreat, forgiveness was on my mind, particularly on the final morning. We were doing a breathwork session facilitated by my friend Rachael, during which I had an experience that stunned and astonished me.

When I meditate or do breathwork sessions, I often go into an imaginative state. I find a sense of clarity and awareness within this state, and it is truly amazing. Often, I receive messages during the meditation or breathwork. This particular time, I did. After the session finished, I asked if I could share what happened with the others in the group. Rachael said, 'Of course.'

I advised the group on the background information for context. I explained that I didn't know the date of birth of my half-sister, Elizabeth. She passed away before I was born and I was not privy to any records specifying her date of birth. Everyone who would know had passed away. What I wanted was to know her date of birth so I could take a moment for her on that date each year, and to put the date on a headstone on her grave. Even giving this information to Births, Deaths and Marriages, they would not tell me her date of birth.

The message that I received during the breathwork session was, 'My birthday was the 18th of September, you silly!'

I still do not know if this date is true, but if it isn't, why did that date come to my mind? The others in the group also seemed just as astonished as I was.

We were all getting ready to finish the session. I went to stand up, and I felt an incredible stabbing pain in my right upper thigh.

I stood, but I could not take a step forward. Pain gripped me. I tried again. I could not put pressure or weight on my leg. I paused and took a deep breath before attempting a third time, and the same thing happened.

I was standing in the same place as the pain tightened and squeezed down my leg whenever I attempted movement. I called out to Rachael, who came straight over. I told her what happened.

'You haven't pulled a hammy, have you?' she asked.

'I don't know, I don't think so,' I replied, as she helped me awkwardly sit back on the ground.

'Is this *your* pain?' Rachael asked. She meant, did the pain belong to me or someone or something else?

'No, I don't think so, I think it's my dad's!'

It was coincidental since I also had the message about my sister's date of birth during the breathwork. It is hard to explain why and how this happened, but I also knew that it was not my pain.

Rachael agreed with me. We both felt that the pain was caused by the past issues with my father, which I had not forgiven him for. Feeling pain on the right side of your body could be representative of unsettled issues with a male, like a father.

Rachael took me through more breathwork exercises. She pushed her hand into where the pain was coming from to help me let it go, to release it as a way of healing.

As she pushed on my thigh, she asked, 'Are you ready to release this?'

'Yes!' I said, yelping with pain.

The pain was sharp, intense, like it was ripping through me. I felt heat radiate over me as if I were standing right beside a raging fire, and my breathing became rapid and shallow. In that moment, on the pain scale of one to ten, with ten being the worst, it would have been a seven or an eight.

After a moment or two of letting it go with my breath, it was weird, but I could feel the pain leave my body. The depth of pain then sank to a two or a three. A moment later, miraculously, it was gone! I could then get up and walk away normally, as if the pain had not been there at all.

It was pain like I had not experienced before, uncanny but real at the same time. Without a doubt, if the pain was caused by an injury when I got up off the ground after the breathwork session, I would not have been able to walk away normally after releasing it with Rachael.

Some may not believe it. But I am a spiritual person, and I believe that the right and left sides of our bodies have different energies that complement each other. The right side harnesses your masculine energy; the left is your feminine energy. When symptoms manifest on either side of your body, it could reveal patterns connected with the masculine or feminine energy in your life. Negative emotions that had been bottled up towards my father surfaced at that moment.

According to MindConnects, 'Negative emotions of anger and unhappiness bottled up towards the parent could be the cause of pain on one side of the body. Acknowledging this and letting go of these negative emotions and forgiveness is the first step to healing[...] This imbalance can be treated through metaphysical treatment like meditation, hypnosis, energy healing followed by renewed way of life.'[18]

As I was having pain in my leg, it could indicate worry about moving forward. I was unable to take that step forward due to unresolved issues with my father. I agreed to release those issues at that moment. However, I could not release all of what I needed; some parts were too deep.

I still suffer periodically with right knee pain, but I have not experienced the thigh pain like I did that day since. That would indicate that I have not entirely healed from the negative emotions.

I am not judgmental of the fact that our brothers were given up for adoption. I understand why they did not tell us. I still find it hard when I think about the fact that they chose not to let us know about Lenny, our eldest brother. Before Lenny found us, our dad tried to stop us from finding Saul. I know my father was afraid.

But we were not fearful, and we did not have to take on our father's fear. Saul was our full-blood brother. We were excited, yet apprehensive and cautious.

Our parents hid what they had been through and did not want to relive it. For that, we tried to be empathetic from the start. What they went through, we are unable to understand fully—we did not live it ourselves. So ...

Can I forgive my father for not telling us that we had two brothers living separate lives from us? Yes, as hard as it has been, yes. Can I forgive him for trying to stop us from finding Saul? Yes. Can I forgive him for not telling us about Lenny (even after we knew about Saul)? Yes.

It has been so hard to let this all go. I still think about it often. But healing from this has meant that I no longer feel the pangs of despair and grief when I do think about it. Instead, I realised we have been so lucky to have relationships with Saul and Lenny, and I am grateful for that.

Can I forgive him for the pain of the things he inflicted upon me and others in my family when we were children? No, I have not forgiven him for that. He was not the father I needed. He took liberties that he should not have. He did not support us, guide us, nor did he do right by us.

I spent a lot of time trying to make my father proud. When I told him I was studying nursing, he said, 'Nurses are born, not made!' I showed him. He had many family members, sisters, and nieces who were nurses. Granted, I had not shown interest in nursing before. After high school, I went into clerical work because I thought I should do something.

I remember sitting with my parents as I tried to determine what I wanted to do after high school. Everything I suggested, my father would disagree with and refer me back to office work. For many years, I was convinced he thought I was not good enough to do the things I wanted or suggested.

In my early adult years, I was consumed with trying to figure out what I wanted to do with my working life. I always knew there was something I should be doing—I was just unable to determine what that something could be. But when I did, I didn't look back.

I allowed myself to be affected by trying to make my dad proud. I don't know why I took this on board, but I did. It wasn't until later in my life that I stopped. I lived in a bubble for forty years of my life. It was not all because of my dad, but he remained a big part of it. I even married a man, my first husband, who I believe was very much like my dad. Don't they say you may end up marrying someone like one of your parents?

I still feel sorrow and longing for what I did not have. I needed a dad, and he didn't give that to me. I do not understand why he was the way he was at his worst. But he did try when he was at his best.

I will remember him for things like how he would lie on the floor watching TV. He enjoyed watching cartoons; that was his childlike side. It was one thing we could do with him. We could also enjoy his favourite Sunday lunch—a fresh loaf of bread, jam and cream. A poor man's scone.

I think forgiveness and healing on this level will take even more intense pain, a ten on the pain scale, and for longer than a moment or two, for me to let it go.

It feels good to begin the healing process, to forgive my dad. However, I am continuing the effort to release, let go, heal and forgive my dad. I am proud of how far I have come in this process, and I am working through it day by day.

Rest in peace, Dad. I hope you found peace.

The idea that my father may still have other deceptions that he did not confide in us brings another layer of complexity, requiring a difficult level of forgiveness. As mentioned before, he may have fathered another son before all of us. Should that prove to be true, I would have to work through another lie.

I suspect he may have fathered other children. Suffice to say, I have ideas and knowledge about this that I will not divulge here. But it is possible that he had affairs during or around his marriages. Should a child have come from those times, they are still our flesh and blood. I hope that they are okay. They are family.

The oldest of my three half-sisters, Lee, was my big sister. She had such an aura about her, a real sense of self-esteem and a smile that could melt. I was in awe of her, and I loved her. I will always live with regret that I did not know that she was overcome with mental pain, and as a result, I could not try to help her. It took me years to come to terms with her passing. Tears well up when I think about her after more than twenty years. I just wish that things had played out differently. I wish I could have been her friend in her time of need.

I would listen to the song she recorded for years after her passing. I'd sing along with tears running down my face. It became hard to listen to.

Her song was originally recorded on a tape. We had that tape redone onto a CD, and since then, my son has copied it onto my computer. I listened to it the other day and I sang along loudly with gusto, tears streaming down my cheeks. No one was in earshot, but even if the neighbours heard, I did not care. It was as if she were right beside me, or we were transported back to the studio when she recorded the song. Even thinking about it now, I can almost see her smiling face looking at me as she sang each word.

I think about the times we shared, the chats, walks to the shops, beach outings, the heart-to-heart talks when I slept in her room, and the honour of being her bridesmaid. I miss her dearly.

The questions remain: Can I forgive myself for not being there, for not being her sister when she needed one? Yes. Can I forgive her for taking her own life? Yes.

I am ten years older than she was when she passed away. I have so many memories, so much to remember her for. I am finally able to forgive myself for not being there for her. I think she would be happy to know that. She would not want me to continually dwell on what might have been.

I cannot judge her for wanting to end her turmoil, and I don't think I ever did blame her; I just felt such intense pain and sadness. But I have to think about the goodness within her heart, and not how it all ended.

My children helped my grief inadvertently with their smiles and our hugs. My son, a toddler at the time, went to daycare, and when I was not at work, I would be home with my then baby daughter. Sometimes, especially when it was just my daughter and me at home, I would hug her. We would sit on the lounge, not moving, with pure sadness as my tears freely flowed down my face. Aloud, I would ask, 'Why? Why?' My daughter was too young to answer, and no one else was there to respond. I do not think I actually wanted answers; I just wanted to express my heartache.

I went through a grief process like no other. I can try to put myself in her shoes, but it's hard because I was not there, and I did not live with the pain and anguish that she experienced.

I will also say that it is the family members and friends left behind who live with their guilt and pain at losing a loved one so tragically. Often, the why question will never be answered. Tears still well up, and I do not think they will ever stop. I can say that, as I have forgiven myself, I can also forgive her. I will always remember her, and I will always have what she meant to me in my heart—that will never change.

I am unsure if some of my father's lies were intended to stay hidden or if they were just part of his attitude that 'The past is in the past.' But when I discovered the true story regarding Julie's adoption, I was completely shocked and bewildered.

I am unable to understand my father and his family's actions. I don't think I will ever. Julie was family, and that should have been all that mattered.

Can I forgive my father and the family for letting Julie be cared for in a home for babies and then adopted at the age of seven? I realise that this is not my issue, but she was my family too. I always knew that Julie was adopted, but I wasn't aware until recently that the papers were signed when she was seven. So, no, I am not there yet.

Julie was eleven years older than me. I do not blame her for becoming estranged from the family. I knew that my sister was out there somewhere, but I did not take steps to find her in my adulthood. I wish I had, but I did not. I will live with that now.

I believe Julie would have had a hard time, especially since her family effectively abandoned her twice. For that, I am deeply sorry. As my father used to say, 'Put yourself in the other person's shoes.' I wish he had put himself in Julie's shoes. If he did, would he have left her in care and agreed to her adoption later?

If I put myself in her shoes, I come up with deep, dispiriting sadness. The sadness of waking up every day without the care of your parents or family. It's so intense, I am unable to comprehend that feeling. That was my father's choice. It was not dictated by society. It should not have happened, regardless of the circumstances.

It would have been hard to have been adopted into another family with different dynamics, especially after spending most of her life in care. Julie lived this.

My brothers were adopted out when they were newborns, aligning, though wrongly, with societal expectations. Julie was a baby, but not a neonate. She was my family. How could anyone do this to her? I know I should let it go, particularly as it didn't happen to me. But I feel for what she went through and the sheer injustice.

Can I forgive myself for not finding her in my adulthood? I wish I had, but maybe I can forgive myself. I certainly cannot change it. I will have to live with that.

I know that she did not try to find us either, but why would she? Not to give excuses for myself, but when she passed away, I would have been starting my own family, and my circumstances would have prevented me from looking for her.

Now, I wish I had. At the time, I didn't value family the way that I do now. If only I had realised it sooner, I could have looked for her and maybe spent time with her. I lost that time. I can never get it back.

I will forever be sad thinking about what she went through. It could, and it should have been so different. But I choose to think of her peacefully, as I imagine her beautiful, long flowing hair and her vibrant smile, the last time I saw her.

When I last saw her walk out of my parents' home, she was sad. I hope that did not last long, that she lived her life filled with happiness and joy. I am sure she did at times, but the knowledge of what happened would have been hard to escape. I hope it didn't negatively shape her life too much. I hope that she is at peace now.

The middle sister, Elizabeth, also had a sad tale, as mentioned. I wish things were different for her. That she lived a longer life. I hope that she would have been able to experience more of life, to love and know her sisters, and to know us. But none of that was possible. Julie was too young to know her, but I do know that Lee, even as a three-year-old, remembered her.

All three of my half-sisters will not be forgotten.

Rest in peace, Lee. Know that you are loved.

Rest in peace, Elizabeth. Know that you are loved.

Rest in peace, Julie. Know that you are loved.

MUM

My mother is still living. I feel intense sadness for the life my mother has had. Had she married someone other than my father, her life could have been so different. Perhaps, though, she would be who she is regardless. She is who she is now.

She was born in a different era, and she has lived with completely different societal issues. Although totally different today, there was no getting away from the community shunning unmarried mothers back then. I am sad for her that that reality did not change before the birth of my brothers.

What both of my parents went through was trauma laid bare—raw, relentless, endless and unbearably tragic. My mother felt the movement of her two oldest children within her for the term of each pregnancy.

Then her two sons, one after the other, were taken from her and forced into adoption. I am sure that her sense of self was lost. My father witnessed this and would have had his own feelings of loss and tragedy. This would change anyone.

It is easy for me to say that they chose to do what they did and become pregnant twice in just over a year. My father would have said that to me had I been in that position. He was brutal with his words when we did what he thought was wrong. But they had to live with these facts, and silently, with little, if any, opportunity to grieve. They would have wondered constantly whether their sons were alive and happy. Living with those thoughts forever in their minds could have been persistently horrendous and heartbreaking. Even things like walking down the street, they would have wondered whether the young boy walking towards them, holding someone else's hand, was their son.

I will forever remain sad for them. Taking a child away from their parents because the child was born out of wedlock should never have happened. Although the government has apologised for past forced adoptions, it will forever remain a dark period in our Australian history.

Now that I know all of that, I do understand why my brother David was the cherished one—the son they were able to keep. The four girls, though, were liabilities to my father. That was how he expressed himself, and there is nothing to excuse his comments. It may have been a lesson for my father to have daughters and cherish them as much as sons. But he did not see it that way. We were not boys, and we were not the boys they had given up. Maybe my mother would have cherished David anyway. Regardless, I know that Jennifer, Cynthia and I were the ones who had to do the housework, make the school lunches and wash our underwear from the ages of seven and eight. David did not have to do that.

But all said and done, my mother made choices when raising her children the way that she did. She was far from maternal. I believe she was not shown love and given hugs by her parents. But we all make our own choices. She could have chosen to treat us differently and love us, even if she didn't feel the love of her parents. That would have been giving more of herself to us in a sense, and she was unable to do that. She missed out on a lot. That is sad. Not only did she miss out on a lot, but so did we.

When she was in the hospital in 2025, she told David and me that 'she failed us.' She was referring to our whole lives—not only did she live with the shame of giving up her sons, but she also lived with the guilt and sadness that she did not give us what we needed. She did not give herself to her children. That must be an enormous realisation for her. My mother has not been one for delving into her emotions; she does not express them. It is good in one sense that she has realised this, but I am sad for her in another sense.

I asked her recently about her childhood. She said she had a 'happy family-based childhood'. I asked her if she had dealt with any trauma that she wanted to speak about. She said no. Those emotions surrounding what happened are so deeply locked away in a vault that she does not see it now. I guess she gained a sense of closure when we found Lenny and Saul; maybe that was enough to put her mind at rest. Or possibly, facing the trauma, even admitting to it, is way too hard. To say she failed us is as far as she could go in acknowledging her trauma.

Effectively, we've known a shell of the woman she was meant to be. When I look at a photo of her taken in teachers' college, I can see the woman she could have been—strong, confident and ready to take on the world. But that did not happen. My father and society changed that, and in the process, it changed all of our lives. I am sad for all of us in that sense. But for my generation, for my siblings and me, we can find a way through. Even if it is not completely evident right now, we can learn to forgive and heal. For my mother, she will not find that, I am pretty confident about that. That is tragic.

This is part of the reason I don't hug my mother. I did after we found out about Lenny, but that is so rare. I do not greet her or leave her with a hug. Nor do I go to her for a hug just because I can. That is my choice, right or wrong. A hug is a sacred thing, full of emotion and love. It can be exactly what you need in a time of need.

For my self-preservation, not hugging her allows me to avoid facing the truth. My mother only hugged me when she'd had a few drinks; it was then that her emotions showed. I wish she could be vulnerable at other times rather than withdrawing most of the time.

But if I hugged her when I wanted a hug, there was a distance, a lack of emotion, without tenderness or love. Perhaps I could try not to be hypocritical and show her the way. Sadly, for her, my avoidance tactic works better for me. At the moment.

I wonder if she would have been the same parent if she hadn't given up her sons. Would she still have lacked that maternal instinct towards her children? The guilt and shame would have been horrendous, but was that the only factor in her not hugging us? Probably not.

From my perspective, our father made her feel inadequate and negative. She allowed herself to be self-conscious and self-critical, and she hid. And then she would project that onto us. Her frustration was triggering, in a way that did not show us how to love and respect her as our mother.

But I will say, with certainty, my mother did the best she could with the hand she was dealt in life.

She has had a hard and sad life. Her father was not present in her life until she was three. She went to boarding school. Then she met her husband, my father, and that changed the course of her life. Maybe she thought she could fix him, as the man who possibly needed help to also be the person he could have been. Unfortunately, she couldn't. It was like a train she couldn't get off.

My mother has always stuck up for my father, whether he was right or wrong, and even after he passed away. That is loyalty at its best. It could be said it was misguided and undeserved. In my eyes, it was. In her eyes, it was not. But to look at it another way, if she did not defend him and his behaviour, then maybe she would have to look at her part in his actions. Maybe then, she would have to accept that she enabled some of his bad behaviour. Was it too hard for her to look at the why and the how? I believe so.

Like my father, not all of the time spent with her was bad. Inadvertently, she taught me to have respect for myself. When I looked through a different lens at her life, I realised that what she had been through with my father could be deemed wrong. She did not have an equal relationship, with respect and love. While my mother would not say that her relationship was unhealthy, I would.

She lived during a time when wives often had to grin and bear it. It was not acceptable for a wife to leave her husband and become a single parent. Because it wasn't common, families often did not know how to support their loved ones who chose to leave their husbands, even in horrendous situations. There were few community or counselling services and no government benefits.

Some women did leave, but it was mostly those who could financially support themselves and their children. For my mum, leaving with five children would have been a huge task. She would not have had family support, which was evident by the way her parents treated her when she became pregnant with my older brothers. So, even if she wanted to leave, she did not.

I am thankful that I left my first husband. I realised that I enabled his bad behaviour. Like my mother, I inadvertently believed I could help him live his best life, but I could not. Unless he wanted to help himself, no one else could help him. I noticed that my children did not smile while we still lived with him. I could not stay in that situation as my mother had. Somehow, I had the courage to walk away with my three children.

I am grateful that I realised that for the sake of my children and myself. I lost, to some extent, respect for my mother for not leaving my father. I did not want my children to disrespect me for the same reason. I do not regret walking away.

I am eternally grateful to my mum for inadvertently showing me the way. I am sorry that she was not also shown the way.

The questions remain. Can I forgive my mother for giving up her sons? Yes. My mother played a part in agreeing with my father not to tell us, and she has continued that even after he passed away. She made choices, albeit influenced by others and societal norms, and she did what she thought was right. I am sorry for her. I won't judge her for that.

Can I forgive her for her part in not telling us the truth about our brothers? Yes, but that was harder to do.

It is easier to be compassionate to my mother than to my father because I am a mother also. Even though I do not understand it all, I forgive her for her part in the lies. Indeed, the pain of finding out we had a brother and then a second brother was intense. It is something that I will not forget, but I can move forward without feeling distress and grief when I think about it. I can heal from that.

Can I forgive her for not being there as my mother? As a child and even an adult, I wanted those hugs. I wanted to be seen, to be shown guidance and given unconditional love. But that did not happen. So, no, I am not there yet.

I understand there may have been mitigating circumstances. She was the parent she knew how to be, and she chose not to show love and attention. But we all make choices. I decided not to raise my children as I had been raised, and so, I became a single parent.

Can I forgive her for not being there when I miscarried? Yes.

Should I be asking this question? I believe so. I would have liked my mum to show concern, but that did not happen. I was unaware at the time that it may have brought her unhappy memories. I sympathise with her for that. With this knowledge, I choose to understand with compassion, rather than judge.

And can I forgive her for the comment she made about David being the only child that they planned to have? Almost.

I am moving forward with the healing, but it's not there yet. My mother could have refrained from saying those words or at least acknowledged that she was happy with all of her children. But she did not. When I think about my children, I would not want them to feel upset because of something I said or did. If that happened, I would try to mend what I had broken. I will always love my children, and I love and respect them and our relationship too much not to work on it if something needs mending.

I visited my mother the day that I was reviewing this chapter. I felt a sense of guilt for writing these words, especially when I wrote that I have not reached total forgiveness for her yet. I do feel so sad for what she has been through. Despite that, I am grateful she gave me life, and peculiarly, she has helped me with my choices and who I am today. After all, she is my mother.

MUM AND DAD

A good friend of mine asked me, 'Could it be that your parents had been unable to see you for yourself because you shone too brightly for them?'

Yes, it could be feasible; it was easier for them not to open their eyes—maybe I gave them a constant reminder of what they had lost.

The truth is, we all suffer. Often in our suffering, we protect ourselves. I felt a lack of safety in my childhood. I built a wall around myself, like a shield, in a bid to feel protected and safe. This also gave me the unhealthy sense of not being worthy of love, so I often looked for it in the wrong places with the wrong people. That is something that I have worked on for myself.

Another avoidance tactic my parents showed me was to work hard. At work, I would push myself and when I got home, I would push myself again to get things done there. It meant that I did not have time to think; I could live in a bubble without being noticed by myself and others.

I did not find time for myself. Essentially, I would not look deep inside myself at what was or is going on—allowing myself to ignore what I was thinking, needing, wanting. My parents taught me this. But I also have to take responsibility for myself. I am learning to find time for myself. How can you give to others if you do not give it to yourself? Much like, how can you love another if you do not love yourself? So, will I heal myself? Yes, in my own time.

My father never looked inwardly, and it would be too hard for my mother to start now. She would have to dig pretty deep to acknowledge and accept what has happened to, or for, her. It is easier to forget or at least try to forget than to face it all head-on.

I followed their logic by not looking at myself or spending time with myself. I am working on that. I now spend time doing the things I enjoy by myself and with my loved ones. Those times are irreplaceable.

When I think about it all, the greatest lessons I have learnt from my parents have contributed greatly to making me the person I am today. I hope that through it all, I am a better wife, mother, sister, aunt, friend and so on. If I had not been through those experiences, I probably would be a different person.

I will always feel bad for Mum and Dad, particularly when they did not heal for themselves and their children. But I am forever grateful to my parents for showing me the way that I should live my life, even if it is different to their way.

GRANDPA (MATERNAL)

My grandfather wanted us to know about our brother. As my aunt told me, he thought, 'That child is going to knock on their door one day, and then they will know it.'

Lenny knocked on our door. We did not have the opportunity to knock on his door, but when he found out that he was adopted, he came looking for us. We knocked on Saul's door once we learnt about him.

On one side of the coin, I wish my grandfather had told us himself. We could then have asked him any questions, and hopefully he would have been able to answer. On the other side, how many answers would he have been able to give us? That I won't know. Facing our questions could have been tough. It definitely would have brought up memories and possibly guilt.

But really, would that have changed anything back then? If we had known years earlier, when our grandfather told our aunt, we could have looked then. We probably would have started our search back then, but it may not have resolved as well as it has.

However it happened, I am glad that we finally know. The journey was worth it. I am so grateful that he passed on the information to our aunt and that she chose to tell us. We would not know otherwise. I am thankful to them for that.

I truly believe that the timing of learning about our brothers was partly due to our grandfather, but it was also divine timing. If we had been told in our twenties, things might have been different.

Can I forgive our grandfather for his part in the adoption of my brothers? Yes. Can I forgive him for not telling us the truth, particularly after my grandmother passed away? Yes.

GRANDMA

My grandmother was instrumental in the adoption of at least one of my brothers. I want to believe that my grandmother actually did tell me about my brother and that I was too young to understand. She may have said, 'Your brother would have loved you.'

But she did not tell me. She lied to me by omission, like my parents. However, it wasn't her story to tell. I do not think it was malicious, but rather, how things were.

My grandmother was so caught up in appearances. You did not cast a cloud over your family; you did nothing that would be frowned upon. It just was not done. If you did, they wouldn't speak about it, but they would cover it up over and over again. That's simply the reality of the times.

My parents paid the price for this, and so too, ultimately, did my brothers and the five of us. It changed the course of all of our lives.

Not only did I feel sorry for my mother going through this, but I also feel sorry for my grandmother. She would not have physically watched her daughter give up her child, but she would have known of the heartache. My grandmother would have known that she was partly responsible for that. She could see how broken my mother was, and yet she could not do anything about it.

My grandmother would have been burdened by societal expectations, but in a different way from my mother. Neither of them should have been held to adhere to such a dark, needless way of treating our young women.

I believe my grandmother would have been troubled by this. How could she not? She lived at a time when society dictated too much of what happened in the lives of ordinary people in extraordinary situations. I feel sorry that she felt pressured by the world she lived in.

Once at a psychic event, I was randomly picked out of the audience. The medium connected to my grandmother. Remarkably, the message from my grandmother was that she was sorry she'd been so worried about what others thought. She said that I should stop worrying about what others think in my life and my family's life. The medium told me that my grandmother said those thoughts, ideas and beliefs needed to stop. How could the medium even know that was so?

It is true, I have always worried about what others think, often to the detriment of myself and my family. If I say that I am going to do something, it is honourable to carry that through. Though in doing so, I can be putting myself or my family last.

It is not selfish to want to spend time doing what we think is right. There is no right or wrong, just a decision based on the moment. Our emotional strength should not be sapped, nor should doing something take a toll on life at home. Sometimes, we are just unable to do what we originally said we would do, and that is okay. Then, we have to learn how to say no. I am learning this now.

I was very close to my grandmother, and even in adulthood, I would turn to her if I needed help with a recipe or a stain in my clothes. I missed the times that I could ring her for advice after she passed away, over twenty-five years ago.

Before she passed, she would say, 'Don't worry about me, don't cry for me, I've had my life, now live yours.' But it was not as easy as that. I missed her terribly.

The question is, can I forgive my grandmother for her part in the adoption of my brothers? Yes. Can I forgive her for not telling us the truth? Yes.

I do not want to hold my grandmother accountable anymore. I forgive her part in all of this.

GRANDMA AND GRANDPA

I always had a soft spot for my grandparents. They did see me. They were good to me. And I loved them for that and much, much more.

I had not been able to go to their gravesites for years. I always thought I would visit, but I could not bring myself to. Then, when we discovered our brothers, I definitely could not go—I was angry and hurt by them. It was something I had to work through.

Last year, Angus and I were staying on the Gold Coast with friends when I decided that I wanted to visit their grave. Weird that I seem to visit graves when I am on holiday. Another visit to a cemetery due to availability. On the way there, we took a wrong turn and ended up at the incorrect location altogether. In the stress of the situation, I was not focusing on what I needed to focus on. I directed Angus wrongly, and consequently, he received his first speeding fine a few weeks later. When we did arrive at the cemetery, it took a little while to find their grave. Out of all the cemeteries I have visited, this one was particularly eerie. I thought that I would feel them there, but I did not. That didn't stop me from talking to them as if they were close, listening to every word.

I asked them, 'Why did you not tell me?'

I told them that we finally knew about our brothers and that we all have good relationships with them. I admitted I was unable to understand their part in the secrets and lies. Ultimately, we had been deceived, but as we did not live in those times, we could not comprehend. As much as I could, I tried to see things from their point of view and the point of view of our parents.

I went on to say that I did not understand how they could banish their daughter and not support her as parents should. Though I realised it must have been one of the hardest things they ever did.

Of course, the answers did not come. Instead, I sensed sadness, regret and anguish. I am unsure if it was their sadness I felt, my own, or both. But I said that I did not want to hold onto what happened when I thought about them. I wanted to think of the good times and the love that we shared.

I told them I had forgiven them. Saying it out loud, while I was standing at their graves, made it all the more real and final, even if no one was listening. It felt good. I did not need or want to feel anymore sadness towards them.

Rest in peace, Grandma and Grandpa. Know that you are loved and always remembered.

GRANDPA (PATERNAL)

My grandfather passed away when I was seven. I do not remember a lot about him, only a few scattered memories.

I have wondered what impact he had on my father. What kind of father was Grandpa? I only remember him as a gentle man, though I did not know him well. If he were a gentle man, my dad did not take after him in that way.

I think my grandparents knew about one or both of my brothers adoptions. When I initially wrote this, I did not think that my grandfather was the type of man to say that my parents would have to adopt the baby out. But apparently, he did say that. At least that is what my father told my mother. Did my grandfather actually say that, or was it another lie that my father told? I will not know the answer to that.

If my grandfather did say it, I think that would have been hard for him to say. I hope in one sense that it was hard for him, not because I want him to have struggled with it—as I am sure he did—but if he did, my ideal of who he was would not be shattered. I want to remember him the way that I do.

The question is, can I forgive my grandfather for his part in the adoption of my brothers? Yes.

MARSIE

I do not know what part Marsie played in the adoption of my brothers. My mother admitted that Marsie and Grandpa knew about the adoption, or at least one of them. I understand Marsie was a Deacon in the Baptist Church. She had a lot of respect within the church, which was massive. As such, a baby born out of wedlock would have been an even bigger disgrace on the family, in the eyes of the church community.

I just do not know why they did not say, 'You must get married now.'

My parents were married not that long after Saul was born. Why didn't they marry before my mum became pregnant, or as soon as they discovered she was pregnant? Then they could have the baby and not go through the adoption process for a second time. I know I did not live then, but that seems to have been an easier solution.

Marsie would not have seen my mum go through this. I do not even know if they knew much about my mum at that stage of my parents' relationship. My dad was pretty good at hiding people and details when he chose to do so. But Marsie would have seen my dad. Did he show anguish at any stage of giving up baby sons? I am sure he did, but I will not know.

The question is, can I forgive my Marsie for her part in the adoption of my brothers? Yes. Can I forgive her for not telling us the truth? Yes.

GRANDPA AND MARSIE

I wish I spent more time with my paternal grandparents. That was not to be. To me, they seemed like a happy, sweet couple who loved their family. My grandmother was a remarkable lady who was capable beyond measure, a woman of great strength, and full of heart. I asked my grandmother one day what the last thing she said to my grandfather was before he passed away.

She paused and said, 'Sweet dreams.'

So beautiful.

I visited the graves of my paternal grandparents in February 2020. When we first found out about our brothers, our parents maintained that Marsie and Grandpa did not know about either pregnancy. So, when I visited their grave, I did not think that I had anything to forgive them for. And so, I did not ask the question, 'Why did you not tell me?'

But I did have something to forgive them for. They knew! Would I have told them how I felt then? Maybe. Marsie and Grandpa were always good to me. I loved them. I have forgiven them for their part in the adoption or adoptions.

Rest in peace, Grandpa and Marsie. Know that you are loved and always remembered.

AUNTY LISA

Aunty Lisa was a big part of our childhood. We spent a lot of time with her and her children. Those times gave us a sense of normalcy with many fun times. The rest of our extended families, on both sides, also played a big part in shaping us. This gave us the idea of what a family filled with love, care and the ability to have fun is like. I am grateful for that.

If Aunty Lisa had not told us about another sibling, we would never have known. She had known for several years before telling us. But really, it happened when it was meant to happen. I do not begrudge that at all.

Holding this secret may have been a burden for her to carry, and for that I am sorry.

Do I forgive Aunty Lisa for telling us or not telling us sooner about our sibling? If there was something to forgive, then yes. But no, there is nothing to forgive.

She merely told us a secret, a betrayal that was held from us. She did what our parents should have done themselves, but they had no intention of telling us. I thank her for her honesty; she was the first one to be honest with us. Her telling us allowed us to know, and then to work through the pain individually as we discovered our family secret. Now we know our brothers. It no longer haunts me that I could walk past my sibling without even knowing if it was him. For that, and her honesty, I will always be grateful.

I will say that I am grateful that I've let go of all I can for the moment. I can now think of those aspects to do with my family members without letting my days be ruined as I have done in the past. But it does not mean that I have forgotten the issues, nor does it mean that I don't have more work to do—because I truly do.

I believe that healing is within all of us; it is an ongoing process. When we heal from one thing, there will inevitably be something else that will follow, another healing aspect in our lives. It might be something from us, or another, but we can deal with it, let it go and move on—if we choose. Before I get to the stage of healing when things happen or as close as possible, I have to continue my healing and forgiveness for the past.

This journey has certainly also been a personal one. I have often had to reinterpret past experiences, find meaning and answers. I have ultimately developed a stronger sense of self during the process. The healing that I have achieved has been emotional, psychological and spiritual. I am thankful for that.

About a year ago, I left a yoga class held by my close friend Jenny. As I hurried to my car, I noticed the eerie street, with little light; the sun had gone down since the class started. Just as I was about to get into my car, in the faint streetlight, I noticed a small piece of paper on the ground beside my car. I thought it was a receipt that had fallen out of my car. So, I bent down, picked it up and placed it in my centre console, and drove home.

The next morning, before driving to work, I noticed the piece of paper from the night before. I picked it up and looked closely at it, and my mouth dropped open. It was not a receipt; it was a square piece of paper that could fit in the palm of my hand. I noticed the background picture first—a peaceful sun rising over quiet water. Then I looked at the words.

It said, 'The day she let go of the things weighing her down, was the day she began to shine the brightest.'

That tiny piece of paper was an amazing stroke of something that came to me that day. It sits stuck to my laptop, now my motto of sorts. The immediate message I received from those words was—by not allowing myself to fully forgive and heal, I am weighing myself down, which in turn does not allow me to move forward and shine.

The part—to shine the brightest—tells me that it is okay for me to be happy; we all deserve that. Forgiveness and healing can be part of my journey towards happiness. Adversity and suffering help us to become the person we were meant to be. I am grateful for the lessons in my life, from my parents and others.

I sincerely hope that as you read these words, you can empathise and see your own path towards healing, forgiveness and ultimately moving forward with happiness, joy and love. You are so deserving of that, now and always. Be open and honest; experience or reinterpret your past and let it go. Seek assistance medically or from those you love, if you need. Ultimately, find the true you, with integrity, empathy and grace. Live, laugh, love and find the joy; we all deserve that.

Let yourself shine! And I will do the same. God bless.

AMENDED FAMILY TREE

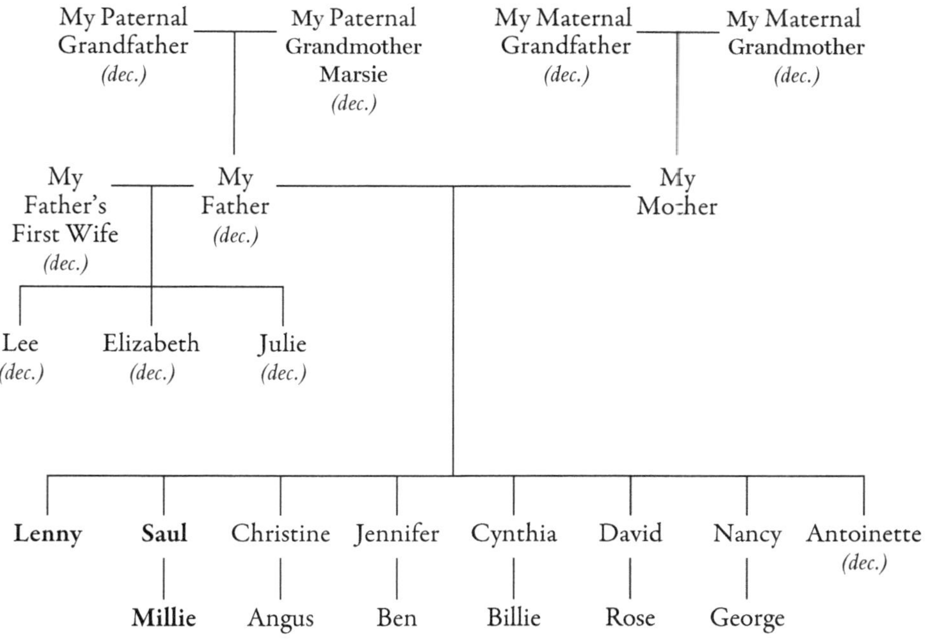

CONCLUSION

My intention for this book was to put my perception out there. It also became my way of shedding light on the fact that an entire family was affected by forced adoption. In my wildest imagination, I did not expect to learn and experience that.

Shame on those who participated in forced adoptions—whoever devised the notion that it was better for the mother and the child—and on those who took the babies simply because they were told to.

It wasn't better for the mother and child, or for the whole family for generations to come!

Initially, my parents were the ones affected in a deeply traumatic way. I do not doubt that. I will not say that what we went through can be compared to what they suffered, because it was not. Even so, and in light of what happened to us as a result, I did not intend to paint my parents in a bad light by writing this book. I have been truthful in what I have written, but I still feel some guilt for writing it.

Had someone said fifteen years ago that all this would happen, I would have scoffed. And yet it did happen.

When I told my maternal grandfather over fifteen years ago that I had separated from my kids' father, he said, 'That's a good thing, you're better off without him!'

That was not the same reaction that my parents received from my grandparents over fifty years ago, when they were disowned for the term of their pregnancy. Then they tried to stop my parents' wedding, partly because my father was a divorcee.

When I became a single working mother of three, the youngest just eighteen months old, times were different. Society did not put restrictions on me. I was fortunate to be able to change my family situation. I was not doing anything wrong in the eyes of society.

Before my separation, my children were not happy, and I was not content in any way. Our living environment on the surface was clean and relatively safe, but my husband at the time was controlling, manipulative and mentally abusive. I knew that walking away would not be the easy way out. But for the love of myself and my children, I chose a single-parent life. I broke the cycle, then and there. I stood tall and started to become me for the first time in my life.

When I became a single parent, it was incredibly challenging on so many levels. I found it hard working my way through debts that were in arrears. I had no money to fall back on, only my part-time wage, as I tried to pay heavily overdue daycare fees, utility bills, car and personal loan debts. I had to go to the charity food services to feed us.

What got me down the most was how my children went through their own mourning process with their parents separating. My siblings and friends were invaluable during the hard times we faced, but the smiles on their faces did return. I am lucky. My children and I have a solid, loving, communicative and respectful relationship every day. I do not regret the hard times; those times have also made us who we are today.

Humbly, through the communication, respect, positivity and resilience that I showed my children, I have helped them and me through those times. I love the people that they have become. I am so grateful for their remarkable and individual qualities. They are amazing.

In life, our parents are the guiding force in how we express and receive our love. My mother was unable to be that for me. Without her role modelling, we were all unable to move forward and build relationships together. Due to the pain she had experienced, she remained closed and emotionally hidden from us. It was not fair that she could not see us as a result, let alone live her life freely and openly.

My mother deserves to be happy. While she loves her children in her own way, she missed out on a lot. For that, I will always remain sad for her.

Above all, I wish that she could and would say sorry.

My father did not answer any of my questions, and now he cannot. His relationship with me was not always marked by love, sincerity or goodwill. I like to think that he would regret that. But in his lifetime, would he have changed it? Possibly, not. Ultimately, he also missed out on a lot.

I, too, wish that he had said sorry.

I am immensely thankful to my siblings, the four of them initially, and their partners and families. I would not be who I am without them. I am grateful that through the support we gave each other, none of us fell into dangerously hard times. We were always able to pull through. I am proud of us all for that.

Discovering Saul and then Lenny were challenging times. We all individually had a lot to work through in our own ways. But throughout it all, we were able to depend on each other for invaluable love, support and friendship. We were boosting our unbreakable bond.

I am eternally grateful for my birth family, which has grown from five to seven children. I now have two older brothers whom I can love, support and be friends with. We are still learning about each other as we develop our connections. It's the future that's important, and I will move heaven and earth just to spend time with them as we create moments and memories together. I am blessed to have this opportunity.

During all of this, Angus has been my rock and my everlasting support. He is the most amazing person that I have ever met. He gave me an ear or a shoulder whenever I needed. I am so grateful for him when I was teary or in a cranky mood, simply when it all became too much. He was patient with my moods, my sadness and my grief. His undivided love gave me strength and the will to move forward.

Our wedding day was one of the most amazing days. It was a day of love and connection that will not be broken. We became a blended family that worked. It was not always easy, but we navigated to where we are today. We have created our own family traditions and these times shared are amazing, beautiful special moments and memories that I would never want to change.

I am lucky to have realised that everything I've been through has given me a greater awareness and appreciation of our children and our relationships with them. I enjoy their hugs, listening to their interactions and their laughter. I love and respect our children even more as I watch and be part of the precious creation of their own families. I am and we are blessed.

What I have learnt throughout this journey has not been limited to relationships. Whilst I am grateful for that, I am also grateful for my personal journey. We all want to be seen, loved and cared for, not just by others but also by ourselves. I can now see myself.

For the first forty years of my life, I say that I was living in my self-protection bubble, just existing. The change in me from then to now has been huge.

Writing this book has enabled me to express my truth. Previously, I had forgotten about the things that hurt because it was easier. Now I no longer choose the easier option. I have allowed myself to open my eyes to things I had forgotten. It has allowed me to examine all of it, sometimes with fear and trepidation, but from a new perspective. I have looked inside myself, even when that has been difficult. I have grown in my understanding of myself. That is something I did not expect.

When we open our hearts to the possibilities, we get to see what happens next. I certainly have opened my heart to myself, my family and my new family. I allowed our lives to be enriched with new memories and precious times that continue to bring us closer together.

I am not so good at expressing kindness to myself. I can do it for others, but not myself. A lot of us are like that. I am learning that kindness, self-love and self-care can be available to us all and that we all deserve it.

Allowing myself to acknowledge that my writing ability has grown is huge. In particular, I no longer believe that I am writing this book as an impostor. I have written my story with my head held high. When I started, I wanted to write my story respectfully with empathy and compassion for my parents. I know that I have pointed out flaws, but that is, from my perspective. I am sure that they would not see it through my lens. I hope that I have remained true to my initial intention to be respectful towards them as I wrote the words in this book. The way that I have written and told the stories within this book will also be interpreted differently by my siblings and you, the reader.

Without discovering our brothers, this book would not have been written. I am so proud to say that I have six siblings. I have three brothers now, and I always had three sisters, as well as three half-sisters. I had a big family before; now it is bigger, with more fun memories and times to be shared.

I'm incredibly grateful for my siblings, each one of them is unique, fun and amazing in their own way. I am proud to call them my brothers and sisters.

I hope you can find some hope in this book. You too can heal and forgive others, and yourself if you need. It is an ongoing journey.

Best wishes to you and thank you for reading my words.

Appendix 1
COURT DOCUMENT FOR MY BROTHER SAUL

Information for: Christine

Regarding your brother,
as taken from the Court Records of the Adoption.

Robert was born in Geelong, on 11 February [....]

The consent to adoption was signed on 16 February [....]

When he was six weeks old,
he was placed in the care of his adoptive parents
in a suburb of Melbourne.

His adoptive parents named him Saul.
He was the second child in the family at the time of the adoption.

His adoptive mother was 35 years old at the time of the adoption
and engaged in home duties.

His adoptive father was 38 years old
and employed as a Baker's Roundsman.

They owned the family home.

They were married for seven years at the time of the adoption,
in accordance with the rites of the Anglican Church.

The adoption was legalised in the Melbourne County Court
on 8 August [....]

SUPPORT SERVICES

If you need, please seek support and/or medical assistance. Don't let yourself or your loved ones endure heartache and grief—it can be lasting and deeply painful.

POST ADOPTION SERVICES
National Services

ALAS Australia Inc: 0417 077 159

Apology Alliance Australia: www.apologyalliance.com

Find & Connect Support Services in your state: 1800 16 11 09

or www.findandconnect.gov.au/support-services/

Care Leavers Australasia Network (CLAN): 1800 008 774 or www.clan.org.au

National adoption helpline: 1800 210 313 (weekdays)

Australian Capital Territory

Benevolent Society New South Wales: 1800 236 762

Family Information Service (Find adoption records and birth relatives): 02 6207 1069

Relationships Australia Canberra and Region: 1300 364 277

New South Wales

Adoptee Rights Australia: www.adopteerightsaustralia.org.au

Benevolent Society New South Wales: 1800 236 762

International Social Service Australia, NSW Special Search Service: 1300 657 843

Origins New South Wales: www.originsnsw.com

Post Adoption Information Unit, Department of Communities and Justice: 1300 799 023 (local call from within NSW and ACT) or 02 9716 3005 (from other states)

Relationships Australia New South Wales: 1300 364 277

Northern Territory

Relationships Australia Northern Territory: 1300 364 277

Territory Families, Adoption: 08 8922 7443 or 08 8922 5519

Queensland

Association of Adoptees: 0417 706 681

Benevolent Society Queensland: 07 3170 4600 or 1800 236 762 or www.pasq@benevolent.org.au

Jigsaw Queensland: 07 3358 6666, which includes the Forced Adoption Support Service Queensland: 1800 21 0313 or www.support@jiogsawqld.org.au

Origins Queensland: 0403 169 509

Post Adoption Support Services, Department of Child Safety, Youth and Women: 07 3097 5100 or 1800 647 983 (free call within Queensland)

South Australia

Department for Child Protection, Adoption: www.childprotection. sa.gov.au/support-and-guidance/adoption-processes or Forced adoptions information and support: 1300 364 277 or the Adoptions team: 03 6166 0422

Post Adoption Support Services (PASS): 08 8245 8100

Relationships Australia South Australia: 1300 364 277

Tasmania

Adoptions and Permanency Services, Department for Education, Children and Young People Tasmania, Forced adoptions information and support: 1300 364 277 or Adoptions: 03 6166 0422

Relationships Australia Tasmania: 1300 364 277

Victoria

Anglicare Victoria: 1800 809 722

Adoption Information Service, Department of Justice, Community and Safety: 1300 194 757 or www.vic.gov.au/past-adoption or www.vic.gov.au/apply-adoption-information

Association of Relinquishing Mothers (ARMS): 0400 701 621

Independent Regional Mothers Group of Victoria: www.independentregionalmothers.com.au/

Origins Victoria Inc: www.originsvic.tripod.com/

Relationships Australia Victoria: 1300 364 277

Uniting Heritage Service: 0402 969 621

VANISH Inc (Victorian Adoption Network for Information and Self Help): 1300 826 474 or www.vanish.org.au

Western Australia

Adoption Research and Counselling Service (ARCS): 08 9370 4914

Adoption Services:1800 182 178

Association Representing Mothers Separated from their Children by Adoption Inc (AMRS): 0468 444 995

Relationships Australia Western Australia: 1300 364 277

INTERNATIONAL SERVICES

International Social Service Australia (family tracing and reunification service, when a family member was adopted in another country): 1300 657 843

FIRST NATIONS AGENCIES/SERVICES

Australians Together: www. australianstogether.org.au/ discover-and-learn/our-history/stolen-generations

Healing Foundation: www.healingfoundation.org.au/

Australian Institute of Aboriginal and Torres Strait Islander Studies (Link-up Services help Indigenous Australians separated from their families): 1800 624 332 or www.aiatsis.gov.au/family-history/ you-start/link or www.aiatsis.gov.au/explore/stolen-generations

COUNSELLING

Beyond Blue: 1300 224 636

Kids Helpline: 1800 551 800

Lifeline (24-hour, 7 days a week, crisis support service): 13 11 14 or www.lifeline.org.au/

Mensline: 1300 789 978

MindSpot: 1800 614 434

National Alcohol and Other Drug Hotline: 1800 250 015

SANE: 1800 187 263

Relationships Australia: 1300 364 277

R U OK?: www.ruok.org.au/

13YARN: 13 92 76

1800RESPECT: 1800 737 732

SUICIDE SUPPORT

StandBy – Support After Suicide: 1300 727 247

Suicide Call Back Service: 1300 659 467

Suicide Prevention Australia: www.suicidepreventionaust.org/

Roses in the Ocean – Peer CARE Companion Warmline: 1800 77 7337

Thirrili – Indigenous Suicide Postvention Service: 1800 805 801

STILLBIRTH AND MISCARRIAGE SUPPORT

Bears of Hope: 1300 11 HOPE or www.bearsofhope.org.au

Miscarriage Australia: www.miscarriageaustralia.com.au/finding-miscarriage-support/support-for-everyone

Pink Elephants (miscarriage & early pregnancy loss): www.pinkelephants.org.au/find-supportRed Nose and Sands (24/7 Support Line): 1300 308 307 or www.supportconnect.org.au/support-options/sands-miscarriage-stillbirth-newborn-death-support-helpline

Stillbirth Foundation Australia: www.stillbirthfoundation.org.au/help-and-support/stillbirth-support-services/

ACKNOWLEDGEMENTS

I'm extremely grateful to Gail Tagarro, The Book Writing Coach. Without her personalised expertise, her support and nurturing of my writing abilities, this book would not have been possible. Your guidance has been so appreciated. Thank you.

I am so grateful to Ann Dettori at Dettori Publishing. Ann, as my Project Manager, and her team—Lucy, Daniela, Jemaja, Renée and Julian, have helped each step of the way without hesitation, giving advice and expertise. Thank you all for your hard work, it is really appreciated.

To my husband, Adam. You have been my rock, my sounding board and my shoulder to cry on. Your wisdom, honesty and loving nature make you the most incredible man I know. Marrying you was one of the luckiest days of my life. You are my soul and my life.

To my children, Zac, Emi and Dan and your partners, you are all such amazing people. I feel so blessed to be your mum. You've helped me discover the kind of mother I wanted to be, and for that I am deeply thankful. I'm so grateful and filled with love for each of you as I witness you be yourselves and live life with joy and love.

To my stepchildren, Alex and Drew and your partners, you are all awesome. Thank you for being amazing every step of the way as

I became your dad's wife, your step mum. Keep being you as great as you are, as you live each moment true to you with love and wonder in everything you do.

The seven of us—Adam, our five children and I—became a beautiful, blended family. It wouldn't have worked without each of you, and I'm deeply grateful for the role you've all played in making it work. As each of your own families grow, I'm thankful to witness and be part of your lives and your beautiful families.

To my parents, Lorraine and Ian, thank you for showing me the way to be me. I hope you find, or did find, healing and forgiveness for all, including yourselves and each other. I hope that you find, or did find, wonder, joy and peace.

To my siblings, Larry, Paul, Jac, Cheryl, Bruce and Nicki, and your partners, Millie, Bob, Rob, Roisin and Grant—thank you all for being the siblings I always needed and wanted. You are all extraordinary, and my heart is full of pride and gratitude. I am proud to say that we are family!

TO THOSE WHO HELPED WITH MY FUNDRAISING

Wow, I'm truly overwhelmed by the support I've received for the fundraising to publish my book. It all began with a Kickstarter campaign that didn't take off, but that would not stop the process. The universe had other plans. Adam, our children, my siblings, and my beautiful friends, Libby and then Megan, who reached out giving help, encouragement and inspiration. My wonderful friends at Kono Kollective Creating Connections always guided me with encouragement, vision and a can-do attitude. I'm so grateful and blessed.

That began a cavalcade of events that we organised:

- Hangi Meal
- High teas
- Meditations
- Sip 'n' paints
- Raffles

The following businesses have helped with the raffles or donations:

- Courtney from the Bronze Edit
- Gail from The Book Writing Coach

- Jane from Haven Yoga and Meditation
- Jules from Julu Photography
- Kiera from Free Spirit Reiki & Healing
- Kono Kollective Creating Connections team
- Michelle Worthington Author
- Trish from Sacred Emotions
- Zoe: www.lomibyzoe.weebly.com

The following individuals helped with donations. Your support has been amazing. I am deeply grateful, with all my heart. Thank you, thank you to:

Adam; Annie; Annette; Bruce and Roisin; Caroline; Caroline and Jake; Cheryl and Rob; Chrissy; Courtney and Zac; Dan and Chantelle; Emi and Chris; Gail; Jac and Bob; Jenny; Jody; Kim; Kylie; Leah; Libby; Liane and Lisa; Linda; Marcia; Megan; Mel; Narelle & Brenden; Nicole; Pat; Paul and Millie; Rejele and Pete; Sharneece; Tanya and Robyn; Teresa; Trevor; Zoe

This journey has not only helped raise the funds needed to publish my book, but it has also brought people together in the most beautiful way. Through these events, around 100 incredible souls have come together through connection, sharing and support. I'm so blessed and deeply grateful to each of you. Your encouragement means the world to me. Thank you from the bottom of my heart.

ABOUT THE AUTHOR

Christine Elizabeth lives in Brisbane, Australia, with her husband, two of her children, and one of their partners. Her other children from their large, blended family also live nearby, and they all continue to enjoy Sunday night dinners and other family get-togethers regularly.

Christine began her career as a nurse, though her childhood dream was to become a journalist. While that dream wasn't realised, she has found great joy in the writing process of this book. Currently, Christine enjoys helping others improve their daily lives through her work as a support worker, meditation and Reiki teacher and numerologist.

The writing experience has been deeply moving, and Christine is already planning her second book.

ENDNOTES

CHAPTER 1

1   Public Record Office Victoria. 2026. *Settlement Schemes (Soldier Settlement)*. Vic.gov.au. 2026. www.prov.vic.gov.au/archive/VF113.

2   Watson, Kathryn. 2021. *What Does It Mean If You Have a Double Crown in Your Hair?* Healthline. Healthline Media. March 2021. www.healthline.com/health/beauty-skin-care/double-crown-hair#what-it-means.

CHAPTER 3

3   Hudson, Grant P. 2018. *The Wisdom of Goethe*. Clarendon House Books. July 28, 2018. www.clarendonhousebooks.com/single-post/2018/07/28/the-wisdom-of-goethe.

CHAPTER 4

4   Thompson, Geoff. 2012. *Given or Taken?* ABC.net.au. February 24, 2012. www.abc.net.au/news/2012-02-24/given-or-taken/3860552.

CHAPTER 5

5   Swain, Shurlee (1985). *A Refuge At Kildare: The history of The Geelong Female Refuge and Bethany Babies' Home*. Bethany Child and Family Support, North Geelong, Vic.

6   Swain, Shurlee (1985). *A Refuge At Kildare: The history of The Geelong Female Refuge and Bethany Babies' Home*. Bethany Child and Family Support, North Geelong, Vic.

7   *Shame*. 2024. Psychology Today. 2024. www.psychologytoday.com/au/basics/shame.

CHAPTER 7

8   Katzenbach, John. 2002. *The Analyst*. Ballantine Books.

CHAPTER 8

9   Australian Government. n.d. "The Privacy Act" Office of the Australian Information Commissioner www.oaic.gov.au/privacy/privacy-legislation/the-privacy-act

10   Victorian Legislation. n.d. "Adoption Act 1984" State Government of Victoria www.vic.gov.au/adoption-legislation-and-standards www.legislation.vic.gov.au/in-force/acts/adoption-act

CHAPTER 11

11   Frost, Robert. 1915. *A Servant to Servants*.

12   Jonathan Safran Foer, Jonathan. 2005. *Extremely Loud & Incredibly Close*. Boston: Houghton Mifflin Harcourt.

CHAPTER 12

13   Jendayi, Sanjo, and Mu Tariq. 2014. *I Now Pronounce You Single and Happy*. DeepRootz.

CHAPTER 15

14   Teaching of Buddha. 1978. *The Teaching of Buddha*. Tokyo: Kosaid Printing Co., Ltd.

CHAPTER 16

15   Owens, Delia. 2018. *Where the Crawdads Sing*. Penguin USA.

CHAPTER 17

16   Southern Living Editors. 2023. "Forgiveness Quotes to Help You Move On." Southern Living. July 6, 2023. www.southernliving.com/culture/forgiveness-quotes.

17   Frederic Luskin. 2003 *Forgive for Good: A PROVEN Prescription for Health and Happiness*. Harper Collins

18   "Pain on One Side of the Body – Metaphysical | MindConnects." 2021. MindConnects | Re-Connecting You with Your Powerful Mind. June 7, 2021. www.mindconnects.org/pain-on-one-side-of-the-body-metaphysical.